ROOTS

A Vegetarian Bounty

ROOTS
A Vegetarian Bounty

Kathleen Mayes
Sandra Gottfried

Woodbridge Press
Santa Barbara, California 93102

Note to the reader

The information in this book is for general information and no responsibility is assumed on the part of the authors or the publisher for its application or use in any specific case or by any particular person.

It is not the purpose of this publication to guarantee any nutritional or medical preparation or the effectiveness thereof. This information is not presented with the intention of diagnosing or prescribing.

Any use of brand names in this book is for identification only, and does not imply endorsement or otherwise by the authors or publisher.

Published and Distributed by

Woodbridge Press Publishing Company
Post Office Box 209
Santa Barbara, California 93102

Copyright © 1995 by Kathleen Mayes and Sandra Gottfried

All rights reserved.

This book, or any portion thereof, may not be reproduced or copied in any manner without the prior written permission of the publisher, except in the case of brief passages incorporated in critical reviews or articles.

Distributed simultaneously in the United States and Canada.
Printed in the United States of America.

Library of Congress Cataloging-in-Publication Data:

Mayes, Kathleen.
    Roots: A Vegetarian Bounty / Kathleen Mayes, Sandra Gottfried
    p.   cm.
    Includes bibliographical references and indexes.
    ISBN 0-88007-206-7 : $14.95
    1. Cookery (Vegetables) 2. Root crops. I. Gottfried, Sandra. II. Title.
TX801.M34 1995
641.6'51—dc20   94-48213
                                     CIP

Contents

Acknowledgments

The authors want to express sincere appreciation for the generous cooperation given by many people in connection with this root guide and cookbook, and especially to the following companies and organizations:

Bishop Museum of Honolulu, Hawaii; Bland Farms of Glennville, Georgia; J.R. Brooks & Son, Inc. of Homestead, Florida; Food Consultants (Hawaii) of Honolulu; Frieda's, Inc. of Los Angeles, California; Idaho Potato Commission of Boise, Idaho; Kyolic, Ltd. of Mission Viejo, California; Landis Valley Museum of Lancaster, Pennsylvania; The Potato Board of Denver, Colorado; University of Maine Cooperative Extension of Orono, Maine; USDA/National Agricultural Library of Beltsville, Maryland; and Uwajimaya of Seattle, Washington.

Graphic credits
Front cover painting and text illustrations are by Janice Blair.

Introduction

THEY'RE BACK!

Exciting news on the culinary scene is that root vegetables are making a comeback and becoming fashionable. Roots are chic and stylish, they're "in," "power" food and versatile — as well as being downright good for you. Leading chefs in trend-setting restaurants and expensive health spas, and private chefs catering to the elite, had practically forgotten the existence of roots; now they're incorporating them prominently into their menus faster than you can say "jicama." They're giving them greater prestige, focusing on their taste, texture and special appeal, finding new and exotic varieties from around the world, or dressing up familiar favorites with sauces of distinction. It's a kitchen revolution! Why? Because roots have a magic that absorbs and balances the flavors of foods and accents the fragrance of herbs and spices. From Manhattan to Marin, from Boise to Baton Rouge, roots are tantalizing the taste buds of diners in the know.

A forgotten food

For years, roots had been the Rodney Dangerfields in the vegetable world — they "got no respect." In spite of today's attention to health and what we should or shouldn't eat, we've tended to overlook some of the healthiest and heartiest of foods. Produce growers had neglected them, cooks had sneered at them, and restaurants had almost forgotten them. We have been happily preparing and enjoying other parts of plants, raw or cooked: we've savored leaves, including trendy ones such as radicchio and arugula; we've chomped down on stems such as asparagus, celery and rhubarb; we've nibbled on blossoms such as artichokes, and on seeds such as grains and nuts. But what of roots? Though we celebrate our diverse ethnic roots and family backgrounds, our culinary roots were left behind and in recent years have numbered only a few. Apart from ubiquitous potatoes, onions, carrots and radishes, many of us had scarcely given a thought to other kinds. We didn't know what to make of them. Noses wrinkled at the mere mention of them. What a mistake!

Give root vegetables a second try and you'll discover what you've been missing. (And when we talk about roots here, we'll be including tubers, edible bulbs, rhizomes and corms — all the wonderful stuff growing beneath and within the good earth.)

Colorful food

The great thing about roots is their variety — more than you ever dreamed of — in all sizes, shapes and colors, of nature's really good food. Admittedly, roots are not much to look at: the Ugly Sisters, you might say, with their wildly strange shapes, rough hairy skins, and unusual earthy smells. But truly, they are Cinderella vegetables, because their unlovely skins hide a multitude of subtle, pleasing flavors, waiting to be revealed by the smart cook. Under the rough, gnarled and knobbly skin, the natural colors are a wonderful artist's palette — the rich purples of beets, deep orange of rutabagas, creamy beige of parsnips, bright pinks of radishes, and the pearly white of jicama. And look at the riot of shapes: perfect spheres, or delicate tapers, or long straight forms such as Japanese daikon, or the incredible lace inside lotus root, all waiting to be sliced, chopped, julienned, shredded or mashed according to your whim or creativity. If you're a newcomer to roots, you may be surprised at their wide range of textures and flavors: the refreshing crispness, the silky smoothness, winelike sweetness or peppery pungency.

Comfort food

Roots humble? Banish the thought! The bottom line is that food should be comforting and companionable, whatever its pedigree, and cheer rather than challenge. After years of relying on restaurants and take-out food, and a succession of boldly aggressive Mexican, blackened Creole, Szechuan and Thai styles, we want to return to homey dishes. We want to cook and entertain at home yet we are busier than, say, ten years ago, and more sophisticated. We don't want to spend hours in the kitchen but still want to strive for the highest standards in cooking. Modern cooks are realizing that roots are comfort foods at their finest: deep-flavored and delicious, familiar yet fresh-tasting, satisfying and soothing, filling but not fattening, hearty but not heavy; they can be styled for contemporary appeal yet still retain old-fashioned goodness.

The revival of interest in comfort food casts a sweet nostalgic light on vegetables nurtured underground. After all, roots reflect the soil and climate in which they are grown, and when roots are organically grown and handled with care, they reward you with some of the finest dishes you've ever tasted.

Year-round food

Whatever month shown on the calendar, roots are perfect all year: we look forward to lovely stews and hearty casseroles thick with rutabagas, celeriac, garlic and parsley root to sustain us winter long. By the time we dig out of winter (whether literally or only metaphorically) and emerge in spring to enjoy the first seasonal flowers, we start to crave lighter vegetables such as leeks and scallions. In summer when we want to tempt appetites wilted by the heat, delicate salad greens can be spiked with peppery roots such as daikon or a touch of horseradish, or given the sweet crunch of jicama; thin sections of water chestnuts go beautifully in a cool aspic accented with chives or other herbs. And how could we get through summer without slices of mild sweet onions on whole-wheat bread for a tasty sandwich? The fall months see us again turning to roots, perhaps marinating beets and carrots in a delicate vinaigrette as a handy make-ahead option, or tossing them into a luscious risotto. With the first snap of frosts, we think of thick chunks of gingerbread, warm and fragrant from the oven, with fresh ginger root in each bite, alongside a glass of cold milk or mugs of newly pressed apple cider, to balance the delightful spiciness.

Versatile food

Roots are more than ingredients for soups and stews. Toss them into pastas and pilafs; make them into crisp fritters or Japanese tempura; cut and slice them for crisp raw chips or whirl them in a processor with blends of favorite spices for uniquely flavorful dips; mash and mold them into patties, and place on whole-wheat buns or into pita-bread pockets with grated Jack cheese and alfalfa sprouts. Give mainstay roots such as carrots and onions a new spin by turning them into salsas, relishes or savory spreads for crusty breads.

Roots can be transformed into superb purées to enhance a dinner dish to satisfy the most fastidious epicurean palate — then later diluted with extra broth or a small amount of cream to create special soups of velvety texture or silky smooth pasta sauces for family suppers. Quick stir-fries are a natural — many roots have Asian origins, and the Chinese, Japanese and Indonesian peoples have been preparing them this way for centuries.

Instead of French fries using potatoes, why not make "root fries" out of celeriac, parsnips, rutabagas or sweet potatoes, as trendy New York chefs are doing? Or create those tiny nests popular in Chinese restaurants: grated roots pressed into special basket-makers (available in Chinese markets), crisply fried then well drained.

Roots make great snack foods. Let's face it, the grazing phenomenon of snacking on small amounts of food between meals is here to stay, and satisfying snacks of crunchy roots (instead of taboo cookies, chips and crackers) can have a positive impact on diets. Raw roots such as jicama, carrots and turnips fit into a healthful eating plan; they're handy as picnic nibbles and party crudités, and taste so good when chilled and crisp, you'll forget that dreary word "diet"! Although your children may be reluctant to eat vegetables, try tempting them with "root fingers" to make them fun food or offering root purées that are easy for toddlers to eat with a spoon.

When introducing family and friends to a new exotic root, or one they "hated" in childhood, coax them with small bites such as intriguing appetizers and canapés — so delicious they'll beg for more! When you get acquainted with the more novel roots, you can appreciate the full range of good things offered by the earth.

Fitness food

Think of roots as the wonders of down under — subterranean treasure chests that are literally storehouses of nutrients. They're not just great tasting, they are great health foods. Consider how much time and energy many of us have spent searching store shelves and box labels for perfect ingredients — food that is low-calorie, has virtually no fat or cholesterol, is high in fiber and complex carbohydrates, rich in vitamins and minerals but low in sodium, and not outrageously expensive. Little did we know that roots fit that description perfectly. How have we let roots get away from us for so long? Roots are returning to the kitchen and being eyed with fresh appreciation as we realize they are packed with nutritious goodies that contribute to maintaining good health. They help you lose weight, prevent heart disease and cancer, lower cholesterol levels, improve digestion and regularity.

So what's in roots? They are loaded with complex carbohydrates (starches and fiber) — a natural healthy source of energy just right for today's active lifestyles. Foods such as roots, fruits, beans, whole-grain breads and cereals provide complex (high-fiber) carbohydrates that the body digests and absorbs more slowly than simple (low-fiber) carbs such as table sugar, honey, candy, cakes and pastries, so roots satisfy us for longer periods of time.

Roots are a neat package of insoluble fiber — cellulose, lignin and hemicellulose — the "roughage" that moves through the digestive system, acting like a kitchen broom. It sweeps the intestines and colon clean of cancer-causing wastes, and swishes stools through the digestive tract, warding off constipation, diverticular pouches in the colon, colon cancers, hemorrhoids and varicose veins. Some studies show that fiber can help lower blood pressure, check the level of fats in the blood and lower total blood cholesterol. Fiber is helpful in weight control: it gives you a feeling of fullness and satiety, but because it's not absorbed into your system, it gives you almost no calories.

Crucifers (so-called because of their cross-shaped flowers) include roots such as kohlrabi, rutabaga and turnip, and they help prevent the growth and spread of cancers in the stomach, intestines and colon.

Eating plenty of roots as well as other vegetables and fruit provides substantial amounts of the anti-oxidants beta-carotene, vitamin A and vitamin C. These disease-fighting nutrients in roots, greens and fruits can reduce the "free radicals" in your body (the toxic substances that roam the body, damaging vital cell structures). Beta-carotene, found in deep-orange produce such as carrots and sweet potatoes, is transformed into vitamin A once it is in your system. (It's worth remembering that while too many carrots may — temporarily and harmlessly — give your skin a yellow tinge, too much vitamin A from a pill supplement can be toxic.) Good sources of vitamin C are found in beets, carrots, jicama, lotus root, parsley root, potatoes, sweet potatoes and turnips.

Other pluses: roots such as beets, celery root, parsnips, rutabagas and turnips supply good amounts of potassium; beets and Jerusalem artichokes offer good sources of iron.

And don't forget the green tops of such roots as beets, leeks, scallions and turnips: they contain some calcium as well as iron, although your body doesn't absorb the iron in greens as well as it does the iron in meat. To boost absorption of iron from vegetables, prepare them in a cast-iron pan or add a source of vitamin C — include tomatoes in the menu, for instance, or drink a glass of orange juice with the meal.

An ancient food

It's interesting to ponder the ups and downs over the centuries in the popularity or disfavor of certain root vegetables. Even the potato wasn't immediately liked in Europe after it was brought back from America by Spanish adventurers. A London newspaper in 1719 observed that potatoes "are of less note than horseradish, radish, scorzoners, beets and skirret." Who now has heard of scorzoners and skirret? It appears that *Scorzonera* is the black variety of salsify still appreciated in Europe, though rarely seen in the U.S.; and skirret crops up only in large dictionaries. And yet in the early eighteenth century these roots were more highly rated than our friend the spud.

Roots are one of the oldest foods known to humans, dating back thousands of years to prehistory, from the time when humans survived by pulling them from the ground to supplement the wild greens, berries, fruit, seeds, nuts and game. When hunts were unsuccessful, primitive families could depend on roots wherever they roamed across continents. Roots were always an important food source because they were protected by the soil from the worst ravages of the weather. And when tribes settled and started farming, roots were among the first plants to be cultivated and improved.

Ancient Romans grew parsnips and onions for their cookpots, and spread them across Europe; Africans have eaten tropical yams and manioc since ancient times; in Asia, radishes, sweet potatoes, ginger and garlic have been valued and transformed into culinary masterpieces by inspired cooks.

In the Americas, long before the Spanish Conquest, Indian tribes prized the thick rootstocks of Solomon's seal, bulbs of the camas and arrowhead, the starchy breadroot and the yampa. Native Americans were growing varieties of sunflowers for their roots (Jerusalem artichokes); Inca food included the tubers of nasturtiums, *ysaño* (that we now enjoy for their ornamental flowers); and Quechuans of the Andes were — and still are — cultivating several hundred potato varieties, skilfully drying and freezing them on mountain tops to store as *chuño* for year-round use.

Roots such as potatoes have played a crucial role in the survival and history of peoples and cultures, helping to avert famine, or were the underlying cause of famine, such as when potato blight caused thousands to starve in eighteenth century Europe when potatoes had been their principal food.

Potatoes in Peril

Potato supplies may soon become scarce, quality may drop and prices rise. Troubling news, nearly 150 years after that devastating assault by Phytophthora infestans on Ireland's potato fields, is that the disease didn't entirely die out, and, as this book is being written, potato growers in many countries are looking with alarm at its recurrence. The fungus has turned into a new chemical-resistant form challenging farmers in the United States, Canada, northern Europe, South America, Japan and parts of Africa. Nobody expects a new famine, since most people eat a diverse diet now, but growers face economic ruin if they fail to watch and protect crops carefully. At the time of writing, international conferences of scientists are pooling information on how the disease affects potatoes, how it spreads from one growing region to another, and what can be done to stop its rampant progress.

The fungus can destroy a potato crop, in fields or in storage, within weeks. Blighted stored potatoes turn a purplish color on the outside and appear shrunken with a corky, reddish-looking rot inside. One infected potato can destroy thousands, and infection can lead to other fungal and bacterial diseases.

Scientists have prepared various strategies to fight P. infestans: some are attempting to cross today's potato varieties with descendants of ancient ancestors, to breed in natural resistance; others are using genetic engineering; and some are examining the use of smarter chemicals for the healthy growth of plants.

There are, however, some peoples around the world, such as the Jains of India and other religious groups, who have been *forbidden* to eat roots or any subterranean foods grown "in the domain of the Devil."

Centuries ago, roots were valued not only for food. With their hairiness and phallic shapes, roots were often used for sacred religious rites, folk medicines and aphrodisiacs; they were believed to have mysterious and special powers, to enhance a man's prowess, to increase sexuality and fertility, and were worn as amulets to ward off bad spirits and curses, or prevent diseases like the Great Plague.

In the days of the first European settlers and homesteaders across America, roots were among the first crops to be planted in the new colonies. Having food to subsist on during the long winters was a great concern and vital to survival. Consequently root vegetables with their ability to keep well for several months were highly regarded and undoubtedly were a basic part of daily meals. The early farmers would carefully store them in outdoor sheds and barns, or under farmhouses in dark "root cellars," to sustain families through the cold months when there was little else to eat. In bins, crates or baskets, the vegetables were sorted and carefully rotated for use, onions were hung from the rafters by their dried tops or laid out on airy racks in attics. Shelves held large jars of pickled beets and onions. You may still have a root cellar under the house if you live in an older home, or you can remember childhood visits to Grandma years ago, when a trip down to the root cellar would be full of mystery, darkness and earthy smells.

But in the 1960s and 1970s, when obtaining vegetables became as simple as a drive to the nearest supermarket, the big producers, growers, shippers and markets ignored roots. With modern refrigerators, freezers and cold storage, we grew oblivious of the seasons and how food arrives in our stores and farmers' markets. We thought we didn't need roots so they lost their importance.

A roots revival

Now roots are back in fashion, we don't have to worry about their availability; most of them are in markets all year — though they always seem to taste especially good in fall and winter when, in some areas of the country, we have fewer choices of fresh produce. However, growing seasons have been extended with the use of plant hybrids, and worldwide trade means more varieties are reaching us from the tropics, other continents and Southern Hemisphere farms and ranches with their reverse seasons. Quantities, quality and selection are better now than they have ever been. What was once considered rare and exotic, such as lotus root, is now sold at large supermarkets and ethnic stores. The more unusual tropicals such as malanga, boniato, cassava and yam from the Caribbean and taro from Hawaii are available in Oriental or Asian markets.

There are some root vegetables, widely grown and eaten in other parts of the world, that are not currently available in our neighborhood of Southern California. When supplies of, say, turnip-rooted chervil, *oca*, *ulluco*, *ysaño* and tropical yam do reach here, we can test and include them in new recipes.

In the meantime, if unusual roots are not in your local markets, ask the produce manager to contact one of these wholesalers:

Frieda's, Inc.
P.O. Box 58488
Los Angeles, CA 90058
Telephone: 213-627-2981

J.R. Brooks & Son, Inc.
P.O. Drawer 9
Homestead, FL 33090-0160
Telephone: 800-327-4833

Choosing roots

One important thing you always want to look for when buying: absolute freshness. Buy the best produce you can find, and if a particular root isn't available or isn't up to standard, choose something else.

Undoubtedly, roots taste best straight out of the garden or soon after purchase, but you don't have to fuss to prepare, cook and eat them the day you get them, unlike leafy vegetables and perishable fruits that quickly wilt, sag or discolor, losing food value.

Although roots such as turnips are among the traditional "cellar vegetables," don't count on prolonged storage, since refrigerators have a higher moisture level than those old-fashioned root cellars. But if you store them properly they will keep, with a few exceptions, for several weeks. See the individual listing for each root for storage details.

Inexpensive food

Root vegetables are economical: "every day" roots widely sold in supers are pennies per serving; even the more exotic types in health-food shops, whole-food stores or ethnic markets are only a couple of dollars per pound and are an inexpensive way to add a gourmet touch to family meals.

If you have a small patch of garden, seed catalogs are crammed with well-tested varieties for you to try growing; producing your own root vegetables is fulfilling and satisfying, and when freshly pulled from the nurturing soil they have a wonderful depth of flavor that adds immeasurably to all dishes.

Preparing roots

Make sure your vegetable peeler and kitchen knives are really sharp. When your peeler becomes dull, toss it and buy a new one. Then peel only the thinnest amount of skin, without removing valued nutrients just underneath. Baby vegetables don't need peeling anyway; simply give them a good scrub with a soft vegetable brush under cold running water to remove the dirt.

Though many roots retain the most nutrients when eaten raw, some have a surprising sweetness after cooking, and there are countless ways to cook them: baking, barbecuing, boiling, braising, microwaving, roasting, sautéing, steaming or stir-frying. Note that some tropicals are toxic when raw; you *must* cook them before eating, to leach out the poisons. This warning is given in the individual listing for the root.

Remember to cook cruciferous vegetables such as turnips and rutabagas in a nonreactive pot — uncoated aluminum, for instance, can intensify odors and create unpleasantly strong flavors. And please don't keep leftover cooked roots for more than a day — unlike wine, they *don't* age well!

The tops of roots such as radishes, turnips and rutabagas are especially good eating; steam them briefly as you would spinach, and dress with a dab of butter or teaspoon of olive oil, or dust them lightly with freshly grated Parmesan cheese.

Don't throw away the water in which you've cooked roots or their tops as it contains valuable nutrients. The cooking liquid is great in soups, stews, for moistening casseroles or creating sauces.

So enjoy your roots! They'll give a special new dimension to meals and menus. They can be unusual, intriguing accompaniments on your dinner plate. Thoughtfully herbed, simply glazed with a little butter, or given a sauce of distinction, roots can be fit for the epicure. Roots are ready and waiting for you and for everyone with the spirit of adventure to experience fresh sensations in cooking and good taste. The world offers a fascinating number of roots for today's cooks and for food lovers of the twenty-first century.

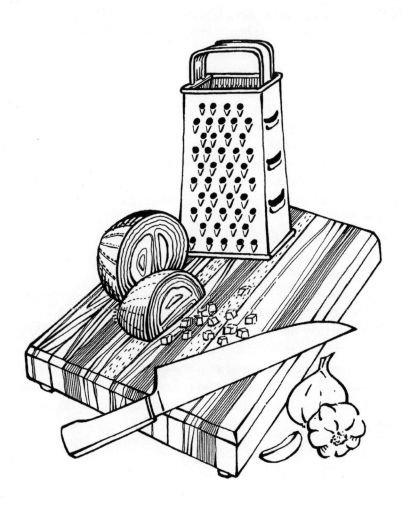

About the Recipes

THE RECIPES that follow include no meat, fish or poultry, but we have used whole eggs, whole milk, whole-milk cheeses and other dairy products. Following current guidelines for good health, we have reduced fat when possible, using nonstick cooking spray for pans and minimal fat to sauté and stir-fry. We have cut back on egg yolks, increased egg whites and, for food safety, specified that all eggs are cooked. We have also used salt sparingly in most dishes because readers may have different taste preferences and sensitivity to sodium.

Traditional root dishes relied on fat for much of the flavoring. Here we utilize fragrant herbs and spices, savory vinegars, tangy lemon juice, zesty garlic and peppers to create new accents and deeper flavors.

If you are a vegan (a vegetarian who doesn't eat eggs, dairy products and honey) or if you are specially concerned about reducing cholesterol or fat, you can substitute other ingredients:

Milk: Switch to nonfat milk or plain soy-milk instead of whole milk. Since these milks are much thinner than whole dairy milk, you may need to make a roux as a thickener in some recipes: for each cup nonfat or soy-milk, add in 1 tablespoon of flour, and blend well.

Butter: Regular margarine can always be substituted for butter and is an option in all recipes.

Cheese: Whenever cheese is called for, you can substitute rennet-free, fat-free cheese or tofu-cheese. Fat-free cheeses are capable of melting smoothly, whereas the tofu-cheeses are not.

Sour cream: Fat-free sour cream, nonfat yogurt or a vegetable-based, non-lactose product will give good results instead of regular dairy sour cream.

Whole eggs: You can use "Egg Beaters" or similar non-yolk egg products in most recipes. You can also use a powdered egg substitute such as "Egg Replacer" in most baking recipes, but not where eggs are the main ingredient, such as in quiche or soufflés.

Nutrition facts: Nutritional values for each recipe have been calculated using the computer software program "Food Processor 2" from ESHA Research. Any values not in the program's database have been provided by manufacturers or wholesalers. If alternative ingredients are listed, the first item only is included in figure; optional foods are excluded.

In figuring analyses, unless otherwise specified, flour is unbleached all-purpose, butter is salted, oil is canola and milk is 4% fat.

If readers follow special diets, and change ingredients, the nutrients will of course differ from the analyses given with the recipes.

The analyses don't include percentages of fat since figures can be misleading when applied to a single recipe rather than to an entire diet. Nutritionists recommend that fat should be no more than 30% of the *total* calories you consume in a day — not of each individual serving.

If you need fat percentages, they are easy to figure: since each gram of fat (whether butter, margarine, oil or shortening) contains 9 calories, multiply the number of grams of fat by 9, then divide by the total number of calories and multiply by 100.

Many of the soups, sauces and gravies in our recipes are created from an all-vegetable stock. When time is short, water flavored with vegetable-stock powder or cube is satisfactory (1 teaspoon powder or 1 cube to each cup water), but creating your own vegetable stock is well worth the effort for the lovely deep cooked-in richness. This stock freezes well.

Basic Root-Vegetable Stock

1½ tablespoons butter or margarine
3 medium carrots, peeled and coarsely chopped
2 medium onions, peeled and coarsely chopped
1 medium turnip, peeled and coarsely chopped
1 medium parsnip, peeled and coarsely chopped
2 ribs celery, chopped
3 quarts water
2 garlic cloves, minced
½ cup fresh parsley, chopped
½ teaspoon each dried thyme, basil and black pepper

1. In a large soup pot, sauté vegetables in butter for about 15 minutes or until golden.
2. Add water, garlic, herbs and pepper.
3. Simmer on low heat for about 1½ hours.
4. Strain and remove vegetables.

(Makes 2½ quarts)

Roots and Recipes

A

Arrowroot

(any of several species of *Maranta* genus, mainly *M.arundinacea*)

Also known as: West Indian arrowroot; Bermuda arrowroot.

History and lore: The plant is probably native to Guyana and Western Brazil, where the root of some varieties was used by native Indians to draw out and absorb poison from arrow wounds. It is now cultivated throughout the West Indies, southeast Asia, Australia and South Africa. The plant produces fleshy tubers from which a finely milled powder is made. Roots are peeled, and the starchy core is grated in water, then the mixture is dried, ground to a powder and purified with several washings. Starches from roots such as arrowroot (and tapioca) have largely been neglected in the United States, but are valued highly in the rest of the world.

Seasons when available: All year.

What to look for when shopping: Superfine pure white powder, sold in small packages and available in natural foods stores.

Nutritional highlights: A source of carbohydrate and protein.

Amount for 4 servings: 1 lb box or cello bag.

How to store: Keep dry in an airtight package on a cool pantry shelf.

Basic prep: Blend the powder with a small amount of water or other cooking liquids to produce a thin paste before adding to soups and sauces, then cook over gentle heat.

Ways to serve: Use arrowroot as a fine quality thickener, for soups, sauces, puddings and desserts,and a light addition to delicate cookies. Since arrowroot has no flavor of its own, it's especially valued for easy digestibility in diets requiring bland food such as meals for sick persons and children.

Arrowroot Cheese Savory

Here's a light luncheon or supper dish ideal for jaded appetites that need tempting. The savory is satisfying and easy to digest. Serve with a small salad and a light gelatin dessert.

2 tablespoons butter or margarine
2 tablespoons arrowroot powder
1 cup whole milk
1 large egg, well beaten
½ cup grated Cheddar cheese
⅓ cup fine dry bread crumbs
¼ teaspoon salt
¼ teaspoon freshly ground black pepper
½ teaspoon dry English mustard powder (if desired)

1. Melt butter in a small pan over gentle heat, add arrowroot powder and mix well.
2. Add milk and beaten egg, and cook until mixture thickens.
3. Add most of the cheese and crumbs, salt, pepper and mustard, beating well all the time.
4. Pour into a greased baking dish, sprinkle with remaining cheese and crumbs.
5. Place under the broiler to brown top.

Makes 2 servings.

Each serving contains about: 420 calories, 16g protein, 25g carbohydrate, 1g fiber, 28g fat, 184mg cholesterol, 789mg sodium.

Arrowroot Lemon Cookies

These thin dainty cookies, with just a hint of lemon, are lovely with a small dish of rich ice cream on a hot summer day or with a cup of herbal tea as a light snack.

1½ cups arrowroot powder
⅓ cup all-purpose flour
1 teaspoon double-acting baking powder
¼ teaspoon salt
½ cup butter or margarine
⅓ cup granulated sugar
Grated rind of ½ lemon
Yolk of 1 large egg
Milk to mix (about ¼ cup)

1. In a medium bowl, sift together arrowroot, flour, baking powder and salt. Cut the butter into small pieces and rub into flour mixture with fingertips.
2. Add lemon rind and egg yolk.
3. Add milk needed to make a stiff dough.
4. Knead to free from cracks, then chill.
5. Roll out to ⅛-inch thickness, prick well and cut into shapes with a fancy cookie cutter.
6. Bake at 350 degrees F for about 15 minutes or until light brown.

Makes 30 cookies.

Each cookie contains about: 65 calories, 1g protein, 8g carbohydrate, 0g fiber, 3g fat, 16mg cholesterol, 61mg sodium.

Fruit and Sherry Elegante

A delicate pudding-like dessert, splashed with a little Sherry, makes a light finale to a dinner party. It can be made well ahead of time, freeing you for other preparations.

½ cup granulated sugar
2 tablespoons arrowroot powder
2 cups whole milk
¼ cup cream Sherry
2 egg yolks, slightly beaten
2 tablespoons butter or margarine
¾ teaspoon vanilla extract
1½ to 2 cups seedless green or red grapes
¼ cup grated coconut

1. In a 2-quart pan mix sugar and arrowroot; add milk and Sherry until well blended.
2. Cook over medium heat, stirring constantly, until boiling.
3. Stir part of the mixture into the egg yolks, then return to pan. Reduce heat and cook for about 30 seconds.
4. Remove from heat and add butter and vanilla extract.
5. Spoon into tall dessert glasses, layering pudding then grapes, ending with pudding. Chill thoroughly.
6. When ready to serve, sprinkle each glass with coconut.

Makes 4 servings.

Each serving contains about: 357 calories, 6g protein, 48g carbohydrate, 1g fiber, 15g fat, 138mg cholesterol, 140mg sodium.

Lemon Cheese Pie

This lemon pie with a texture close to cheesecake has a tangy filling to make it a refreshing dessert in summer.

    Crumb crust for a 9-inch pie (see recipe below)
    1⅓ cups granulated sugar (divided)
    ¼ cup arrowroot powder
    1 cup water
    ⅓ cup freshly squeezed lemon juice
    1 teaspoon grated lemon peel
    2 large eggs, separated
    1 (8-oz) package cream cheese, room temperature

1. Prepare pie crust and set aside.
2. In a medium pan, mix 1 cup of the sugar with arrowroot. Stir in water, lemon juice, lemon peel and beaten egg yolks. Cook, stirring, over medium heat until thickened.
3. Remove from heat and blend in cream cheese.
4. In a separate bowl whisk egg whites until soft peaks form. Add remaining ⅓ cup sugar. Fold into lemon mixture.
5. Turn into pie crust and chill.

Crumb crust (for one 9-inch pie)

    1½ cups graham-cracker crumbs (approx. 11 crackers)
    ⅓ cup granulated sugar
    ⅓ cup melted butter or margarine

Combine mixture and press into pie-plate bottom and up the sides.

Makes one 9-inch pie, about 10 servings.

Each serving contains about: 318 calories, 4g protein, 43g carbohydrate, 1g fiber, 16g fat, 84mg cholesterol, 195mg sodium.

Banana Arrowroot Muffins

Bring fragrant oven-warm muffins to the Sunday brunch table — and watch them disappear! Arrowroot makes the muffins fine-textured with a slight chewiness, and the bananas give natural sweetness. Serve with apricot preserves or simply with unsalted butter.

> 2 large bananas, well mashed
> 2 large eggs
> 1½ cups unbleached all-purpose flour
> ½ cup arrowroot powder
> ⅔ cup granulated sugar
> 1 teaspoon *each* salt and baking soda
> 2 tablespoons melted butter or margarine

1. Position rack in center of oven, preheat oven to 375 degrees F and coat muffin wells with nonstick cooking spray, or grease lightly.
2. In a 2-quart bowl beat bananas until smooth and whisk in eggs until light and fluffy.
3. Sift together flour, arrowroot, sugar, salt and baking soda, and gradually add to egg mixture. Add melted butter and gently stir to blend thoroughly.
4. Spoon batter into prepared muffin wells until ¾ full.
5. Bake at 375 degrees F for 25 to 30 minutes until tops are golden brown and a toothpick inserted in centers comes out clean.
6. Remove from pan and cool slightly. Serve warm.

Makes about 12 2½-inch muffins.

Each muffin contains about: 163 calories, 3g protein, 32g carbohydrate, 1g fiber, 3g fat, 40mg cholesterol, 277mg sodium.

B

Beet
(*Beta vulgaris*)

Different types: There are four types of beet: 1) the table or garden beet, 2) the leaf beet (also known as Swiss chard, silverbeet or spinach beet) grown for its wonderful-tasting leaves, 3) the sugar beet, with the root grown as a source for sugar, and 4) the mangold (or mangel-wurzel) as a feed for livestock.

History and lore: Four hundred years ago, the beet was valued in folk medicine as a cure for jaundice, a bone salve and an emetic. Beet juice was recommended as a soothing remedy for festering wounds and infectious bites.

Beets originally grew wild around the Mediterranean. Cultivation of the leaf beet dates from prehistory in cool regions and during cooler seasons. Greeks and Romans enjoyed the leaves of the plant, and it wasn't until the beginning of the Christian era that they discovered the roots were also good eating.

You can find mangel-wurzels listed in "heirloom" seed catalogs, where they are described as "primarily for cattle feed." A few centuries ago, however, these large beets were eaten by many European peasants when they lived close to their livestock, and survived long hard winters by sharing food and sleeping quarters with their animals.

Beets are still popular in many regions: Hungarians put beets into dumplings, Scandinavians add beets to meatballs, Midwesterners mix apples with beets, and the Pennsylvania Dutch make beet pickles as part of their "seven sweets and seven sours."

But there's no doubt people today are polarized about these roots: they adore them or shun them completely. When you do eat large quantities, be forewarned that their strong water-soluble red pigments can turn urine red. Before you phone the doctor, recall what you ate for dinner!

Seasons when available: Most of the year, with a peak in June and July.

What to look for when shopping: The root of the table beet is thick and fleshy, with shapes varying between globe-like to long and tapered. If leaves are still intact, they are a good indicator of root freshness; they should be bright and unwilted. Look for firm, smooth roots with no cuts or blemishes. Buy small or medium-sized beets; avoid large ones that may be woody, even after long boiling, and shriveled ones that will be too old.

Skin and flesh colors are usually dark purplish red. Farmers' markets may sell white varieties or gold ones the color of sunshine with buttery sweetness the reds can't match. Italian Chioggia beets with white/red candy-stripes are ultra-sweet, to entice the "never-eat-beets" person.

Nutritional highlights: More natural sugars than any other vegetable. A good source of calcium, iron, potassium and vitamin A.

Amount for 4 servings: Five medium, about 1¼ pounds.

Basic prep: Cut off all but 2 inches of stems and leaves as soon as you get home. If left on, they'll draw out flavor from the roots. Store greens in a plastic bag in the refrigerator, and use within a day or two. Refrigerate roots, unwashed, in a plastic bag, and cook within five days.

How to cook: Sauté the lush tender greens, without stems, as a separate dish with a little olive oil, lemon juice and garlic. Leaves are also delicious raw in salads.

Cook red beets whole, leaving on root tips and a couple of inches of stem, so color won't bleed. Whites and goldens don't bleed.

Steam or simmer in salted water: small beets for about 30 minutes, larger ones for about one hour. Or try roasting small beets: place in a casserole, drizzle with walnut oil or olive oil and bake an hour or more in a 325 degree oven until tender.

Ways to serve: Be gentle with beets: a little salt and pepper on the cooked roots; a dab of butter, a pinch of sugar, or a dash of cardamom spice. Or toss cooked slices or dice in a sweet-sour sauce, in plain yogurt, a raspberry vinegar or mild vinaigrette. Serve hot golden beets with butter and chopped candied ginger; or white beets thinly sliced and dressed with cream and a sprinkling of nutmeg. Many youngsters are reluctant to eat a beet, but blend one with a comfort food such as mashed potatoes, and the novelty of fuchsia-pink spuds is irresistible!

Evelyn's Beet Borscht

Colorful, full-flavored beet borscht originated in Russia (the word deriving from borshch, *Russian for "cow parsnip," the original base for this soup). Other Russian versions of borscht use spinach or cabbage; and in Hungary cooks make a white-color borscht using cherries and a milk or cream base.*

Both of Sandra's parents were born in Russia, and this soup was a staple at home, served hot in winter, cold in summer. When Sandra's mother served it hot, she always put a boiled potato in the middle of each bowl, and the smetana *(topping) was a dollop of sour cream.*

    2 lb medium to large beets (7 or 8), scraped and sliced
    1 medium onion, peeled and sliced
    Juice of 1 lemon
    ¼ cup granulated sugar
    1 teaspoon salt
    8 cups water
    2 large eggs
    8 small red potatoes, boiled, skins removed
    ½ cup sour cream

1. Put beets in a large soup pot with onion, lemon juice, sugar, salt and water. Cook until beets are tender, about 15 to 20 minutes.
2. Drain liquid and set aside.
3. Beat eggs until frothy.
4. Put beets, onion and 2 cups of beet liquid in a food processor, and purée.
5. Put rest of liquid back in soup pot with purée. Very slowly add a ladle of soup into the eggs, whisking constantly.
6. Add egg mixture to the soup, and simmer gently for 5 to 10 minutes. Do not boil, or eggs will curdle.
7. Serve hot, with a boiled potato and a dollop of sour cream in the center of each bowl.

Makes 8 servings.

Each serving contains about: 238 calories, 6g protein, 45g carbohydrate, 5g fiber, 4g fat, 59mg cholesterol, 359mg sodium.

Gingery Beets

The lemon, ginger and dry mustard give this colorful beet side-dish a delightful sweet-sour flavor. If using beets of several colors, cook red beets separately.

> 1 lb beets (red-striped, gold, white or regular red), leaving on 1 inch
> of tops
> 1 tablespoon butter or margarine
> 1 tablespoon unbleached all-purpose flour
> 1 tablespoon lemon juice
> 2 tablespoons brown sugar
> ¼ teaspoon dry mustard
> ½ teaspoon ground ginger

1. In a medium saucepan cover beets with cold water and boil for about 20 to 30 minutes or until tender.
2. Let cool, drain, reserving ½ cup of cooking liquid.
3. Remove skins. Cut beets into julienne strips or slices.
4. Make sauce: in a small saucepan blend flour with butter and brown lightly. Add reserved cooking liquid and seasonings. Cook 3 to 5 minutes.
5. Stir in beets and serve warm.

Makes 5 or 6 servings.

Each serving contains about: 76 calories, 1g protein, 13g carbohydrate, 2g fiber, 2g fat, 6mg cholesterol, 73mg sodium.

Tangy Beet Mold

This gelatin salad not only tastes good, it looks lovely on the table.

1 (1-lb) can sliced beets
1 envelope plain gelatin
½ cup water
3 tablespoons lemon juice
1 tablespoon red-wine vinegar
2 tablespoons finely minced onion
½ cup finely chopped celery
1 tablespoon prepared horseradish

1. Drain beets and reserve ½ cup liquid. Set aside.
2. Sprinkle gelatin over water in a small pan to soften.
3. Add lemon juice, vinegar and ½ cup beet juice. Heat, stirring constantly, until gelatin is completely dissolved. Cool about half-hour.
4. Blend in onion, celery and horseradish.
5. Chill until slightly thickened.
6. Fold in drained beets. Pour into a three-cup mold or individual molds.
7. Chill several hours or overnight.

Makes 6 servings.

Each serving contains about: 33 calories, 2g protein, 7g carbohydrate, 2g fiber, 1g fat, 0mg cholesterol, 219mg sodium.

Beet Date Bread

A wonderful bread to make on a rainy day. A little time-consuming, but well worth the effort.

    3½ cups warm water (divided)
    10 pitted dates
    2 tablespoons yeast granules (dry active yeast)
    2 tablespoons cooking oil
    8 cups whole-wheat flour
    2 cups grated raw beets

1. In food processor or blender, purée dates with 1 cup of the water. Place in a large bowl.
2. Add remaining water (2½ cups) and stir.
3. Sprinkle yeast over top of mixture. Let sit in a warm (not hot) place for about 15 minutes until yeast is bubbly.
4. Add oil and flour. Mix well.
5. Cover bowl and let sit until double in volume.
6. Divide dough into two even parts. To each part, add one cup of beets.
7. Knead well, adding flour when necessary to absorb moisture from the beets.
8. Spray or grease two loaf pans. Put dough in prepared pan and leave to rise a second time, doubling in size.
9. Bake at 325 degrees F for 1½ hours.

Makes 2 large loaves, about 32 slices.

Each slice contains about: 121 calories, 4g protein, 25g carbohydrate, 4g fiber, 1g fat, 0mg cholesterol, 8mg sodium.

Blush Cake

The beets give this cake a nice moistness, color and natural sweetness, enhanced by the honey. A cream-cheese frosting is the perfect topping.

1¼ cups all-purpose flour
1 cup granulated sugar
¼ cup cocoa powder (not processed cocoa drink-mix)
1 teaspoon baking soda
2 large eggs
½ cup grated cooked red beets
1½ tablespoons honey
1 teaspoon vanilla extract
½ cup plus 2 tablespoons butter or margarine, melted
¼ cup milk
Cream-cheese frosting (see recipe below)

1. Mix flour, sugar, cocoa and baking soda in a large bowl. Set aside.
2. With an electric mixer, beat eggs, beets, honey, vanilla, butter and milk.
3. Add dry ingredients to egg-mixture, and beat on medium speed for 2 minutes.
4. Pour into a sprayed or greased 8-inch square cake pan.
5. Bake at 350 degrees F for about 40 minutes.
6. When cake is cool, spread with cream-cheese frosting.

Cream-cheese frosting (about 3 cups):

1 (3-oz) package cream cheese
1 tablespoon milk
1 teaspoon vanilla extract
2½ cups confectioners' sugar

1. Blend cheese with milk and vanilla.
2. Gradually add sugar. Beat until smooth. If too thick, add more milk, 1 teaspoon at a time.
3. Spread on cooled cake.

Makes one 8-inch square cake, about 12 servings.

Each serving (including frosting) contains about: 332 calories, 4g protein, 51g carbohydrate, 1g fiber, 14g fat, 70mg cholesterol, 218mg sodium.

Can't-Be-Beat Pie

The beets blend well with the fruit in this pie — an unusual combination that can convert your "never-eat-beets" friends.

>   Pastry for a double-crust 9-inch pie (see recipe below)
>   ¾ cup grated cooked beets, well drained
>   3 cups peeled and sliced Pippin or green apples
>   1 cup peeled and sliced pears
>   3 tablespoons frozen orange-juice concentrate, thawed
>   ½ cup brown sugar
>   ½ cup granulated sugar
>   4 teaspoons lemon juice
>   4 teaspoons tapioca
>   ¼ cup honey
>   2 tablespoons butter or margarine

1. Prepare pastry and divide dough in half. Roll one half and line pan.
2. In a large bowl mix remaining ingredients except butter, and place in pie crust. Top with butter.
3. Roll out top crust and place on filling. Trim. Pinch edges together and press with tines of a fork to make a simple design. Poke a couple of small holes in top crust to let steam escape.
4. Bake at 425 degrees F for about 35 minutes.

Pastry (for one 9-inch double-crust pie):

>   ⅔ cup butter or margarine
>   1½ teaspoons granulated sugar
>   ¼ teaspoon salt
>   2 cups unbleached all-purpose or pastry flour
>   3 tablespoons ice water

1. Mix all ingredients. Chill in freezer for about ½ hour.
2. Divide dough into two. Roll one half and place in 9-inch pie pan.

Makes one 9-inch pie, about 8 servings.

Each serving contains about: 466 calories, 4g protein, 73g carbohydrate, 3g fiber, 19g fat, 49mg cholesterol, 266mg sodium.

Boniato

(Ipomea batata)   See also Sweet potato.

Also known as: Batata; Batata dulce; *Camote*; Cuban sweet potato; White sweet potato. Polynesians refer to it as *Kumar* or *Kumara*. Related to the familiar sweet potato Americans enjoy at Thanksgiving; boniato refers to the tropical variety.

History and lore: All forms of the sweet potato originated in Central America; they were later (from about 1000 B.C.) cultivated in Peru and Colombia. Some historians believe early voyagers venturing from South America across the Pacific may have taken this vegetable to Polynesia, because islanders know it as *kumar* and *kumara*, names thought to have derived from the Indian Quechuan language.

Boniato is the Spanish name for tropical sweet potatoes. When the word was first noted in the Caribbean in 1537, it probably was used as an adjective to describe something sweet and good (as opposed to poisonous or harmful), but by the eighteenth century the word had evolved just to mean the good-tasting sweet potato.

Seasons when available: Year-round, though scarce in February and March. Generally sold by Hispanic markets catering to immigrants from the Caribbean; may be difficult to find in West Coast stores.

What to look for when shopping: An oval or long tuber with rough skin that may be reddish, pinkish or purplish, with flesh that is off-white to light yellow. Look for boniatos that are firm, free from mold, blemishes or signs of sprouting. Boniatos are prone to bruising and rapid deterioration — so check carefully.

Nutritional highlights: Rich in vitamin A and potassium; some vitamin C and protein.

Amount for 4 servings: About 2 lb.

Basic prep: Keep at room temperature, in a single layer, in a paper sack or airy basket — never in the refrigerator. Sweet potatoes do not store well, so plan to use boniatos within three or four days of purchase.

How to cook: Wash and scrub boniatos. If peeling, remove skin with a sharp knife or potato peeler and cut into large chunks; submerge pieces in water immediately to avoid discoloration. While boiling, keep chunks covered to prevent flesh from turning gray; they will be tender in about 25 minutes.

Boniatos can also be prepared with skins intact and removed after cooking. They can be baked, fried, mashed or puréed, microwaved, scalloped or added to soups.

Ways to serve: Use them as you would regular sweet potatoes, but season lightly as boniatos are mild in flavor and less sweet. Mash with cream or butter, salt and freshly ground pepper; or whirl in a processor with a little apple juice.

Caribbean Potato Boats

A simple way to introduce this lovely vegetable to your family. Choose well shaped tubers that will make an attractive serving at the dinner table.

2 lb (4 small) boniatos
3 tablespoons butter or margarine (divided)
2 tablespoons milk or cream
2 tablespoons orange juice
½ teaspoon salt
¼ teaspoon freshly ground black pepper

1. Scrub tuber skins and dry well. Rub skins with 1 tablespoon of the butter (to keep skins soft).
2. Place in a baking dish and bake at 400 degrees F for about 1 hour.
3. Cut each boniato in half lengthwise. Scoop out flesh, leaving a ¼-inch thick shell.
4. Whisk the pulp with the remainder of butter, milk, orange juice and seasonings. Refill shells, mounding neatly, and return to baking sheet.
5. Reheat at 450 degrees F for about 10 minutes. Serve hot.

Makes 4 servings.

Each serving contains about: 357 calories, 3g protein, 62g carbohydrate, 3g fiber, 9g fat, 24mg cholesterol, 379mg sodium.

C

Carrot
(*Daucus carota*, var. *sativus*)

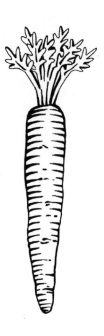

History and lore: This native to Afghanistan, India and eastern Russia spread to China and flourished around the Mediterranean and northern Europe. Archeologists working in caves in Switzerland have found ancient stores of carrot seeds dating from 3000 to 2000 B.C. To Greeks and Romans, carrots were "love medicine"; and mothers in the Middle Ages thought eating this phallic root was immoral, warning their daughters of the dangers of loose sexual desires. But when the Dutch introduced the carrot to Queen Elizabeth I, she pronounced it agreeable and the ladies of the court adorned their hair with the fernlike tops.

Centuries ago, people enjoyed the sweetness of carrots perhaps even more than we do today. At the beginning of the 18th century, after the British Navy had blocked supplies of West Indian cane sugar from reaching Europe, chemists found it possible to produce a percentage of sugar from carrots as well as beets. Beet sugar is still made, of course, but carrot-sugar was subsequently dropped as being uneconomical. The Irish still quaintly refer to this natural sweetness as their "underground honey."

Although we think of a carrot as essentially orange in color, this form was developed relatively recently in the 17th century by Dutch growers. In the New World, the carrot didn't exist until British colonists brought seeds from their cultivated plants; now naturalized carrots are common roadside weeds in North America.

Seasons when available: All the year.

What to look for when shopping: Slender firm carrots with smooth surfaces and deep orange color; other colors can be white, yellow or even purple flesh. If tops are attached, be sure they are bright and perky, to indicate freshness. Old carrots will be woody and tough, and lack flavor. Carrots can range from globular to long, with the ends blunt or tapered.

Nutritional highlights: Carrots have more natural sugars than any other vegetable except beets. The deeper the orange color, the more beta-carotene they contain. Carrots are good sources of potassium and calcium, and are low in sodium.

Amount for 4 servings: About 1¼ lbs.

How to store: Remove leaves immediately you arrive home, as they leach out moisture from roots. Well-wrapped in plastic bags in the vegetable bin, carrots will keep several weeks. Reseal bags carefully after each use to be sure remaining carrots don't dry out. Carrots will turn bitter if stored close to apples.

Basic prep: Baby carrots need only a good scrub with a stiff brush under running water. Scrape older ones, remove ends and any green areas. Leave carrots whole, cut lengthwise, or crosswise into ¼-inch slices. Heat 1 inch salted water to boiling and add carrots. Cover and heat to boiling and cook until tender: 20 minutes for whole; 15 minutes lengthwise strips; 5 minutes for shredded. Or microwave: 6 whole carrots in a 1½ quart covered dish take 10 to 12 minutes.

Ways to serve: Buttered, with salt and pepper. Sprinkled with snipped parsley, mint, chives or chopped green onion. Highlight the natural sweetness by seasoning them with sweet spices such as ginger and cardamom. Or by contrast, add slightly sour herbs such as tarragon or dill.

Bangkok Carrot Soup

People living in the tropics know that a refreshing chilled soup for lunch or dinner makes a delicious cooler on a hot day. So when the temperature sizzles, make this one in early morning or overnight and it will become your summer-time favorite. Mock-chicken bouillon is sold in most health-food or specialty stores: mix 1 teaspoon bouillon for each cup of water.

> 1 lb carrots, scraped and cut into chunks
> 1 medium onion, chopped
> 1 garlic clove, minced
> 2 tablespoons butter or margarine
> 1 teaspoon curry powder
> 4 cups mock-chicken stock (divided)
> 1 cup canned coconut milk
> Salt and pepper to taste

1. Cook carrots in a soup pot with boiling water for about 15 minutes or until tender. Drain, and place in food processor.
2. In a small saucepan sauté onion and garlic in butter until transparent. Add curry powder and cook another two minutes.
3. Add curry mixture to the carrots with one cup of the mock-chicken stock and purée.
4. Pour into soup pot, add remaining stock, coconut milk, salt and pepper. Simmer about 3 minutes to blend flavors.
5. Chill soup thoroughly for several hours before serving.

Makes 4 servings.

Each serving contains about: 245 calories, 4g protein, 18g carbohydrate, 5g fiber, 19g fat, 16mg cholesterol, 1229mg sodium.

Favorite Carrot Ring

Sandra's family always ask for this traditional favorite at Thanksgiving; it makes an attractive colorful centerpiece for the holiday table. You can prepare the mixture the day before, as far as filling the ring mold; cover and refrigerate overnight, then bake an hour or so just before serving. Fill the ring-center with garden peas and surround the platter with fresh steamed vegetables such as half-ears of corn, squash, and cauliflowerets.

3 sticks (1½ cups) butter or margarine
1 cup brown sugar, firmly packed
4 large eggs, separated
3 cups finely grated carrots (about 1 lb)
2 tablespoons cold water
2 tablespoons lemon juice
2 cups unbleached all-purpose flour
2 teaspoons baking powder
1 teaspoon baking soda

1. Cream butter with brown sugar. Add egg yolks and beat together until thick.
2. Add grated carrots, water, lemon juice, flour, baking powder and baking soda. Mix thoroughly.
3. Whisk egg whites until stiff peaks form; fold into carrot mixture.
4. Lightly coat a 3-quart ring mold or Bundt pan with vegetable cooking spray, and turn mixture into pan.
5. Bake at 350 degrees F for 1 hour.
6. Remove from oven and let set about 5 minutes before loosening edges with knife. Turn upside down onto a large round serving platter.
7. Garnish with vegetables.

Makes about 12 servings.

Each serving contains about: 386 calories, 5g protein, 37g carbohydrate, 1g fiber, 25g fat, 133mg cholesterol, 394mg sodium.

Carrot Soufflé

Soufflés always have an air of elegance and yet they are economical dishes. Serve with a crisp green salad and a glass of chilled white wine.

  3 large eggs, separated
  4 tablespoons butter or margarine
  2 tablespoons unbleached all-purpose flour
  ¾ cup whole milk
  1 teaspoon granulated sugar
  ¼ teaspoon dried thyme
  ¼ teaspoon grated nutmeg
  1¼ cups finely grated carrots (2 or 3)
  ½ small onion, finely chopped

1. Lightly coat a 1-quart soufflé dish with vegetable cooking spray; set aside. Preheat oven to 350 degrees F.
2. In a small bowl, beat egg yolks; set aside. In a separate bowl, whisk whites until soft peaks form; set aside.
3. In a medium pan, melt butter over medium heat. Add flour and stir until smooth. Gradually add milk and stir until smooth and thickened. Remove from heat.
4. Add sugar, thyme, nutmeg and beaten egg yolks.
5. Fold in carrots, onions and egg whites to egg-yolk mixture. Put into prepared baking dish.
6. Bake at 350 degrees F for 35 minutes or until set.

Makes 4 servings.

Each serving contains about: 227 calories, 7g protein, 12g carbohydrate, 2g fiber, 17g fat, 196mg cholesterol, 200mg sodium.

Carrot and Eggplant Spanakopita

A popular dish in Greece is Spanakopita, a type of pie made with filo dough and usually filled with a spinach mixture. Carrots are innovative and give the dish a new spin. When shopping for feta cheese, the domestic style is less strong and less expensive. Filo dough can be found in the frozen food section of most supermarkets.

4 cups peeled and diced eggplant
2 tablespoons minced onions
2 garlic cloves, minced
3 tablespoons olive oil
3 cups grated carrots
¼ cup fresh parsley
1 teaspoon dried thyme
2 large eggs, well beaten
1 lb feta cheese
½ cup melted butter or margarine (divided)
1 lb filo dough, thawed for about 2 hours

1. In a large pan sauté eggplant, onion and garlic in olive oil for about 5 minutes. Add carrots, parsley and thyme, and cook another 5 minutes. Set aside.
2. Whisk eggs in a medium bowl and add crumbled cheese. Set aside.
3. Brush a 13 x 9 x 2-inch pan with a tablespoon of the melted butter.
4. Unwrap filo sheets, smooth out creases and divide into two, allowing one-half for the bottom and one-half for the top. Lay first sheet in pan and brush with warm butter. Continue till half the filo is gone, buttering between each sheet.
5. Stir eggplant-carrot mixture into egg-cheese mixture and spread over filo dough. Layer the remaining filo, buttering each piece in between until finished. Roll and tuck all the filo around the inside edges of the pan. Don't cut any off. Top with remaining butter.
6. Bake at 350 degrees F for 50 minutes. Cut into squares.

Makes about 8 servings.

Each serving contains about: 532 calories, 16g protein, 46g carbohydrate, 4g fiber, 31g fat, 135mg cholesterol, 1090mg sodium.

Chocolate Carrot Cake

This chocolate cake, with carrots to give delicious moistness, can be topped with your favorite frosting or glaze, or simply dusted with a little powdered confectioners' sugar.

1½ cups finely grated carrots, packed
¾ cup granulated sugar
½ cup cooking oil
1 cup boiling water
1½ cups whole-wheat flour
½ cup unsweetened cocoa powder
1½ teaspoons baking powder
½ teaspoon ground cinnamon

1. Position rack in center of oven, preheat oven to 350 degrees F and lightly coat an 8-inch square pan with nonstick cooking spray.
2. In a large bowl mix carrots, sugar and oil. Pour boiling water over mixture. Stir together, then set aside.
3. In a separate bowl sift and stir dry ingredients, and add to carrot mixture. Mix well. Pour batter into prepared pan.
4. Bake at 350 degrees F for 35 minutes.

Makes 9 servings.

Each serving (without frosting) contains about: 260 calories, 4g protein, 35g carbohydrate, 5g fiber, 13g fat, 0mg cholesterol, 97mg sodium.

Cassava

(Manihot esculenta)

Also known as: Manioc; Mandioca; Tapioca; Yuca (pronounced YOOkah). (Although sometimes incorrectly spelled Yucca, it is not the same genus as the bayonet-leaved plants in the Agave family).

History and lore: Cassava originated in Brazil (the scientific name *Manihot* is the Indian word for the root), and is now cultivated throughout South and Central America, the Caribbean, Africa, Asia and South Pacific. In the United States it is grown for immigrants who have come from these areas of the world, and who shop in neighborhood markets for foods they would eat in their home country. Cassava is also delighting gourmets in America who want to add an exotic touch to their cuisine.

Cassava goes into *sancocho*, a traditional stew in South America and the Caribbean prepared with other root vegetables and salted meats; East Africans simmer cassava with beef, onions, tomatoes, coconut milk and chile peppers; Nigerians enjoy cassava with salt herring; and Pacific islanders put grated cassava into dumplings and breads.

Cassava roots are ground into meal and processed into pellets, flakes, granules, flour and products such as *tapioca*; probably the most common use of cassava in the United States is in the form of tapioca. When cooked with water, tapioca swells and thickens to become a pale translucent jelly, valued for thickening liquids, broths, soups, puddings and juicy pies.

Seasons when available: All the year, in ethnic markets carrying imported fresh vegetables, and occasionally in large supermarkets. Tapioca in packages is always available in grocery sections.

What to look for when shopping: Narrow roots similar to sweet potatoes, but covered with brown bark-like peel; roughly 8 inches long and 2 inches diameter. Choose roots without spots of black mold or greenish-black mildew. Inside flesh should be hard, dense and white like coconut, with a sticky consistency and a sweet buttery flavor.

Nutritional highlights: Vitamins A and C, calcium, iron and potassium.

Amount for 4 servings: About 2 lbs.

How to store: Fresh cassava needs cool storage, but not in the refrigerator. Use promptly, within a week. Or wash, peel and cut them into chunks and wrap tightly. Cut cassava can be refrigerated for up to 24 hours, or stored in the freezer for several months. (Ethnic markets sometimes sell the tubers in this way.)

Store packages of tapioca on a cool pantry shelf.

Basic prep: *This root must be cooked before eating. It is poisonous when raw.* The bitter odor is due to the roots' prussic acid content, but the variety grown for U.S. markets is not harmful when cooked. Scrub each tuber and peel with a sharp knife before using. Flavor after cooking is similar to soft potato, with a sweet butteriness.

Although a staple starch in tropical countries, cassava may cause some people with delicate digestions to suffer upset stomachs. When trying it, take only small portions at first.

Ways to serve: Use in soups and stews. Cassava can be boiled, sautéed, fried or used in well-seasoned, spicy and picante sauces. Cut cooked tubers into fingers for appetizers: fry the sticks in olive oil with cloves of garlic and sprinkle with fresh chopped cilantro. Or boil it and then purée. Or grate the cooked roots and toss into cakes, breads and puddings.

Islanders in the South Pacific make tapioca-like desserts baked with coconut milk or grated coconut, topped with slices of mango, papaya or pineapple.

When ripe fruit is juicy and must be thickened for a simple dessert, add 2 tablespoons tapioca to every 5 or 6 cups of fruit or berries. For thickening fruit-pie fillings: in a 9-inch pie, add about 3 tablespoons tapioca.

Cassava Au Gratin

Cassava (or yuca) is sweeter and more dense than potato. Here it gives a creative spin to a favorite side dish.

2 cups prepared cassava (see below)
2 tablespoons butter or margarine
2 tablespoons unbleached all-purpose flour
1 cup milk
1 cup grated Cheddar cheese

1. To prepare cassava: scrub tubers, peel with a sharp knife and slice fairly thick. Plunge into boiling water and cook about 10 to 12 minutes until slightly tender. Drain. Should be 2 cups.
2. Spray a shallow baking dish with nonstick cooking spray or grease lightly.
3. In a small pan melt butter, add flour and stir until well blended. Gradually add milk, stirring constantly until thickened. Remove from heat and add cheese.
4. Put a little cheese sauce on bottom of dish. Add cassava slices. Cover with remainder of sauce.
5. Bake at 350 degrees F for 30 to 40 minutes, until bubbly.

Makes 4 servings.

Each serving contains about: 352 calories, 13g protein, 37g carbohydrate, 5g fiber, 18g fat, 53mg cholesterol, 273mg sodium.

Rhubarb Yogurt Pie

When rhubarb is in season, buy plenty, to make good use of its lovely tart-sweet flavor. In this pie the yogurt gives the filling a creamy smoothness, thickened with tapioca.

> Pastry for a 9-inch pie-shell (see recipe below)
> 3 cups chopped fresh rhubarb
> 1 cup plain yogurt (or sour cream)
> 3 tablespoons tapioca
> 1 large egg, well beaten
> 1½ cups granulated sugar
> Strawberries for decoration (optional)

1. Prepare pastry, and fit into pie pan. Fill with chopped rhubarb, and set aside.
2. In a medium bowl, whisk yogurt with tapioca, egg and sugar. Pour mixture over rhubarb.
3. Bake at 425 degrees F for 15 minutes. Reduce heat to 350 degrees F and bake for 30 to 35 minutes until filling is set.
4. Decorate with fresh strawberries, if desired.

Pastry (single crust for one 9-inch pie)
> ½ cup (1 stick) margarine
> 1 teaspoon granulated sugar
> ⅛ teaspoon salt
> 1¼ cups unbleached all-purpose or pastry flour
> 2 tablespoons ice water

Mix all ingredients. Chill in freezer for about ½ hour. Roll out and trim to fit 9-inch pie pan, giving edges a decorative finish with fingertips.

Makes one 9-inch pie, about 8 servings.

Each serving contains about: 366 calories, 5g protein, 60g carbohydrate, 2g fiber, 12g fat, 27mg cholesterol, 218mg sodium.

Lazy Apple "Pie"

This "pie" is for those times when you're hungry for a homemade apple dessert but don't want to fuss with making pastry crust.

3 cups peeled and sliced tart apples
½ cup brown sugar
½ teaspoon cinnamon powder
2 cups boiling water
⅓ cup quick-cooking tapioca
¼ cup granulated white sugar
⅛ teaspoon salt

1. Preheat oven to 350 degrees F and lightly coat a baking dish with nonstick cooking spray.
2. Place sliced apples in dish. Mix brown sugar and cinnamon together and sprinkle over apples. Bake at 350 degrees F for 15 minutes.
3. Meanwhile, in a medium saucepan mix boiling water with tapioca, sugar and salt. Cook and stir over medium heat for 5 to 10 minutes, until tapioca is transparent.
4. Pour tapioca mixture over apples and continue baking about 20 minutes, or until apples are tender.
5. Serve warm, topped with whipped cream or ice cream.

Makes 6 servings.

Each serving contains about: 161 calories, 1g protein, 42g carbohydrate, 1g fiber, 1g fat, 0mg cholesterol, 52mg sodium.

Chocolate Tapioca

Chocolate pudding is comfort food at its finest. Top each serving with a dollop of whipped cream and decorate with fresh fruit in season.

¾ cup granulated sugar
⅓ cup unsweetened cocoa powder
3 tablespoons quick-cooking tapioca
2⅔ cups milk
1 large egg, slightly beaten
1 teaspoon vanilla extract

1. Mix sugar, cocoa and tapioca in a medium pan. Blend in milk and egg. Let stand about 5 minutes.
2. Cook mixture over medium heat, stirring constantly until it boils. Remove from heat and stir in vanilla.
3. Pour into dessert glasses or bowls. Chill until ready to serve. (Top each glass with a piece of plastic wrap to prevent skin forming on pudding.)

Makes 4 servings.

Each serving (without topping) contains about: 305 calories, 8g protein, 55g carbohydrate, 2g fiber, 8g fat, 75mg cholesterol, 147mg sodium.

Celeriac

(Apium graveolens, var. *Rapaceum)*

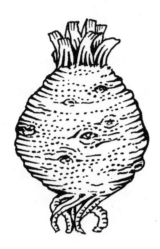

Also known as: Celery root; Knob celery; Turnip-rooted celery.

History and lore: Regular celery is native to the Mediterranean countries, and spread across Europe and the Middle East. The Greeks and Romans used it as a flavoring, and the ancient Chinese thought it valuable as a medicine. Celeriac came upon the scene when European botanists developed this variety of branch celery from wild-growing plants in the 17th century, and within a century it was popular standard fare. But in the United States, celeriac is one of the most overlooked vegetables.

Even today, celeriac is well known in Northern Europe, Germany, Holland and Poland, where cooks rely on it during winter months. A chunk of *Sellerie*, is always included in the "German soup green," a little packet of vegetables ready to drop into hearty soups; and *céleri-rave rémoulade*, grated celery root with herb mayonnaise, is commonly served as an hors d'oeuvre or salad in French bistros.

Seasons when available: August through May. Wait for fall before celeriac is in its best form and flavor.

What to look for when shopping: The size of a small cantaloupe, a lopsided sphere, embossed and channeled, patterned with crevices, whorls and wayward rootlets. Creamy-white in color and often muddy, the root is certainly ugly with a characteristic pungent smell, but don't be put off. Choose small to medium-sized roots that are firm, not spongy. The texture is crisp. Flavor is similar to celery, and some say there's a walnut-like taste.

Nutritional highlights: Low in calories, and a good source of vitamin C, potassium and fiber.

Amount for 4 servings: About 1 lb.

How to store: Wrapped in plastic and stored in the refrigerator, celeriac will keep for about one week.

Basic prep: Can be used as a raw or cooked vegetable. Trim off any stalks; they're excellent in soups and stews but have a stronger flavor than celery.

Wash the root well. If using it raw, peel away skin and side shoots (with a stainless steel knife, as iron discolors the root). After peeling, store in a bowl with water and lemon juice till you're ready to use it. Celeriac can be diced, sliced or cut into thin julienne. You can also cook celeriac first, then peel it.

Ways to serve: Crunchy celeriac makes a crisp accent in a simple salad when julienned and tossed in a vinaigrette dressing with chopped tomatoes, thinly sliced carrots and coarsely grated beets. Use celeriac in salads, soups, stews and stir-fries. Season with the root's herbal kin, parsley or dill. Innovative chefs on the cutting edge in smart restaurants are now serving the *céleri* chip — thinly sliced and deep fried.

Celeriac Salad

This salad is delicious on its own, or it can be served with greens, cold pasta or rice.

1¼ lb (2 medium) celeriac
6 tablespoons olive oil
3 tablespoons white-wine vinegar
1 teaspoon granulated sugar
1 teaspoon caraway seeds
½ teaspoon salt
2 garlic cloves, minced
⅓ cup mayonnaise

1. Wash and peel celeriac root; cut into matchstick size pieces and place in a glass bowl. Set aside.
2. Make marinade: Mix olive oil, vinegar, sugar, caraway seeds, salt and garlic. Pour over celeriac and cover.
3. Leave at room temperature for about 2 hours, stirring occasionally.
4. Just before serving, drain off and discard marinade. Add mayonnaise.

Makes 4 servings.

Each serving contains about: 207 calories, 2g protein, 11g carbohydrate, 7g fiber, 18g fat, 11mg cholesterol, 325mg sodium.

Purée of Celeriac

The French make wonderful purées and this one is no exception. You can add or subtract any of the vegetables below, and still have great success. Mock-chicken bouillon can be found in health-food stores.

Serve this lovely dish on cooked, cooled, artichoke bottoms, with a clear soup and a crisp green salad for an elegant luncheon or supper.

2¾ cups mock-chicken broth
1 cup diced celeriac
3 to 4 cups diced carrots, turnips, rutabagas or parsnips (mixed)
½ cup butter or margarine
1½ tablespoons brown sugar
¼ teaspoon white pepper

1. In a large pan, heat mock-chicken broth to boiling.
2. Add vegetables and cook until tender, about 35 minutes. Strain.
3. Transfer vegetables to food processor and purée.
4. Add butter, brown sugar and pepper.
5. Coat baking dish with vegetable cooking spray or grease lightly.
6. Place purée mixture in baking dish, cover, and heat at 350 degrees F until just warmed through. Remove cover and continue baking another 5 minutes.

Makes 6 servings.

Each serving contains about: 211 calories, 2g protein, 17g carbohydrate, 5g fiber, 16g fat, 42mg cholesterol, 736mg sodium.

Celeriac Casserole

The celery flavor is distinctive yet mellowed by the sauce, and the root gives a nice crunch to this simple colorful dish.

    4 lbs celeriac (3½ cups after slicing)
    ¼ cup butter or margarine
    2 tablespoons unbleached all-purpose flour
    1 cup milk
    4 oz shredded Cheddar cheese (divided)
    ½ lb fresh mushrooms, sliced
    ½ green bell pepper, chopped
    2 tablespoons pimiento (canned or in jar)

1. Prepare a 1-quart baking dish with nonstick cooking spray, and set aside.
2. Scrub and peel celeriac, and slice thinly.
3. In a medium pan cook celeriac in butter, covered, for about 15 minutes or until tender.
4. Add flour and milk, and stir until thick and bubbly. Cook 2 minutes more. Remove from heat.
5. Add about ¾ of the cheese and stir until melted.
6. Put in prepared baking dish and stir in mushrooms, bell pepper and pimiento. Sprinkle with remaining cheese.
7. Bake uncovered at 350 degrees F for about 20 minutes or until cheese topping melts and bubbles.

Makes 6 servings.

Each serving contains about: 267 calories, 10g protein, 25g carbohydrate, 15g fiber, 16g fat, 46mg cholesterol, 402mg sodium.

Celeriac and Tofu

Tofu picks up the flavor of whatever food it is combined with, and here it blends beautifully with the assertive taste of the celeriac and the tangy dressing. This is a main dish to be served on a bed of cooked rice or noodles, along with steamed vegetables. Start the meal with a chilled gazpacho soup and finish with a light dessert.

2 cups celeriac cut into julienne (matchstick-size strips)
2 cups firm tofu cut in cubes
¼ cup chopped red onion
1 egg yolk
2 tablespoons balsamic vinegar
2 teaspoons fresh lemon juice
½ cup olive oil
1 garlic clove, minced
1 teaspoon Dijon-style mustard
1 tablespoon crushed dried oregano
½ teaspoon sugar
Salt and pepper to taste

1. Combine celeriac, tofu and onion in a medium bowl.
2. Combine all other ingredients in food processor or blender, and whirl until smooth. Pour over celeriac mixture, and toss to coat well. Cover.
3. Chill for at least 1 hour.

Makes 4 servings.

Each serving contains about: 418 calories, 13g protein, 19g carbohydrate, 13g fiber, 35g fat, 53mg cholesterol, 299mg sodium.

D

Daikon

(*Raphanus sativus*)   See also its cousin, Radish.

Also known as: Chinese radish; Chinese white turnip; Japanese radish; Korean turnip; *Lo bok*; Oriental radish.

History and lore: The two Japanese characters that make up the word daikon mean "great root," and this may be Japan's most important vegetable. It's a staple in Chinese cooking, and at Chinese New Year banquets it is included in special dishes served to guests and family. Cultivation of radishes goes back to early human history; they were well known to ancient Chinese, Egyptians, Greeks and Romans.

Folk healers and scientists have all believed in the outstanding medicinal and nutritional qualities of raw and pickled daikon. Eaten raw, daikon is used throughout Japan to complement the taste of oily foods and help in their digestion. Traditional Japanese restaurants put grated daikon in tempura dip to help digest any oiliness, and serve shredded daikon alongside raw fish to digest the protein.

The Japanese make traditional pickles with daikon: in rural areas they hang up the roots by their leaves, to dry them in the autumn sunshine. After they are dried, the daikon is packed into large crocks with layers of sea-salt and aged for months — even years.

Seasons when available: Year-round. Fresh daikon is always available in Oriental food stores, and often in natural-food stores and larger supermarkets. Asian markets may also sell pickled daikon in jars.

What to look for when shopping: This is one of many different radishes originally cultivated in the Orient, of the same botanical group as our familiar red-colored ball-shaped radish. Daikon is a large, white, cylindrical radish about 2 inches in diameter and up to 18 inches long. The Chinese type, *lo bok*, is shorter, thicker, more fibrous and with a stronger flavor than the Japanese variety. Daikon is sometimes sold with its green leafy top, which can be an indication of its freshness. Choose firm, smooth roots with a luminous gleam, not a flat opacity which indicates long storage. Taste is a sharp peppery-hot radish flavor; texture should be crisp.

Nutritional highlights: Low in calories. Good sources of vitamins A and C, calcium and potassium.

Amount for 4 servings: About ½ lb.

How to store: Remove green tops, if any. Wrap root closely in plastic and store in vegetable crisper, up to one week. Oriental radishes are not good keepers, as they soon become flabby and insipid, so plan to use them promptly.

Daikon is also available dried: the sealed package keeps well when stored in a cool dry place. Reconstitute by soaking in lukewarm water for one hour before draining well and sautéing.

Basic prep: Wash and shred or dice daikon. Chill in ice water for 30 minutes before serving, to make it crisp and crystal white. Cooked daikon loses some of its crunch and becomes less peppery. The green tops can be braised, steamed, blanched or added to soup.

Ways to serve: Raw daikon can be shredded, diced or sliced, then tossed into relishes, salsas, salads and platters of crudités. Daikon is often carved into edible flowers as lovely garnishes for Japanese dishes. Simmer thick slices of daikon in soups or add them to stir-fries. Dip them in soy sauce or a pickle marinade to serve as a relish or side dish.

Daikon and Eggplant Soup

This smooth simple soup goes beautifully with a salad and crusty French bread for a satisfying lunch or dinner.

> 8 cups vegetable stock (see page 20), or vegetable bouillon (1 teaspoon or 1 cube for each cup water)
> 1½ lbs Japanese eggplant, ends removed, sliced thickly
> 1 daikon, peeled and quartered
> 2 garlic cloves, peeled
> Salt and black pepper to taste

1. Bring vegetable stock to boil. Add eggplant and daikon, and cook about 10 minutes over medium heat until vegetables are tender.
2. Purée vegetables with garlic in food processor. Return to soup pot and warm over low heat.
3. Ladle into soup bowls and serve hot.

Makes 4 servings.

Each serving contains about: 127 calories, 5g protein, 26g carbohydrate, 8g fiber, 4g fat, 9mg cholesterol, 270mg sodium.

Daikon Stir-fry

This daikon dish is quick and simple to make when you're rushing to get dinner on the table after a long working day. Serve alongside hot cooked brown rice or a bowl of vegetable soup.

2 to 3 tablespoons peanut oil
4 cups shredded daikon
1 scallion, minced
1 tablespoon soy sauce
1 teaspoon sugar
½ teaspoon freshly ground black pepper

1. Heat oil in wok or fry pan. Add daikon when oil is hot. Stir-fry for about 3 to 4 minutes, mashing down daikon firmly to ensure complete even cooking.
2. Remove from heat and sprinkle with minced scallion, soy sauce, sugar and pepper. Mix together.
3. Reheat one more minute, pressing mixture again so that it resembles hashed-brown potatoes. Serve warm over hot cooked rice or crispy noodles.

Makes 4 servings.

Each serving contains about: 87 calories, 1g protein, 6g carbohydrate, 2g fiber, 7g fat, 0mg cholesterol, 278mg sodium.

Pickled Daikon

Store these colorful pickles in the refrigerator for at least a week, to let the flavors mature and develop, then use them within 2 weeks. Serve them as a side dish or garnish, or instead of a salad. Jars of these pickles make lovely gifts for friends.

1 large daikon radish (about 1 lb), peeled
3 large carrots, peeled
1 large cucumber
4 ribs celery
8 scallions
4 oz fresh ginger root, peeled
1 large green bell pepper, seeded
½ large red bell pepper, seeded
½ large yellow bell pepper, seeded
1 (3½-oz) package enoki mushrooms
Pickling Liquid (see recipe below)

1. Prepare vegetables in a large bowl: cut daikon, carrots and cucumber into matchstick-size pieces; thinly slice celery, onions and ginger root; cut bell peppers into ½-inch dice; clean mushroom stems and pull apart.
2. Half-fill a large soup pot with water. Bring water to boil.
3. Add vegetables. Remove from heat and let vegetables stand uncovered for 2 minutes. Drain well.
4. Place vegetables in sterilized jars. Prepare pickling liquid and, while hot, pour over vegetables to cover them completely. Screw lids tightly on jars and refrigerate about a week.
5. Serve chilled.

Pickling Liquid

3 cups granulated sugar
3 cups white vinegar
1½ cups water
1 teaspoon salt

Combine all ingredients in a medium saucepan. Cook over medium heat until liquid boils. Remove from heat.

Makes 1½ to 2 quarts (about 14 ½-cup servings).

Each serving contains about: 206 calories, 1g protein, 53g carbohydrate, 2g fiber, 1g fat, 0mg cholesterol, 182mg sodium.

F

Fennel

(Foeniculum vulgare, var. *dulce)*

Also known as: Sweet fennel; Florence fennel; Finocchio. There are two types of fennel: Sweet Fennel, grown mainly for its swollen "bulb" at the base of the plant; and common fennel from which we get the lovely anise-flavored seeds used as an herb. Here we have the bulb variety.

History and lore: Fennel probably originated in countries around the northern shores of the Mediterranean, Greece, Italy and France. The Greek word for fennel was *marathon*; where the famous battle took place was so-called because the area was overgrown with the plant. According to Greek myth, knowledge came to humans from Olympus in the form of a fiery coal contained in a fennel stalk.

Ancient Romans enjoyed a number of varieties of fennel in their foods including flat breads generously seasoned with fennel, cheese and olive oil; and in a later century, Alexander Dumas wrote that in the streets of France *"it is not rare to meet common people with a bundle of fennel tucked under the arm, making of it, with a little bread, their lunch or dinner."*

Seasons when available: Late summer through early spring.

What to look for when shopping: A pale-green feather-topped vegetable, with celery-like stems and enlarged bulb-like base of overlapping layers. Look for fresh green leaves and crisp compact greenish-white bulbs. The flavor, similar to licorice and anise-seed, is less pungent; it becomes incredibly sweet after cooking.

Nutritional highlights: Low calorie; a source of vitamin A, calcium, potassium and iron.

Amount for 4 servings: 2 medium bulbs, about 1¼ lb.

How to store: Wash it well, trim the bottom and top, removing any bruised outer pieces. Wrapped in plastic and refrigerated, it should keep for a week, but is best used within a few days.

Basic prep: Cut fennel into neat strips for eating raw in salads and salsas; slice the bulb ¼-inch thick before steaming, sautéing or stir-frying; or cut it into quarters, remove tough core, drizzle with olive oil and bake for about 35 minutes until tender.

Ways to serve: The aromatic vegetable is delicious served Italian style: raw with crumbly-fresh Parmesan cheese, or with a mild soft goat cheese and a few green olives. Fennel sautés beautifully along with artichoke hearts, zucchini, tomatoes, sweet bell peppers and fresh thyme in a Provence-style *ratatouille* that can be served hot or cold. Or the chilled cooked vegetable can be simply dressed with a spoonful of fresh lemon juice and extra virgin olive oil, and topped with snipped chives.

Fennel Tomato Soup

This hearty soup, thick with vegetables, is perfect for those nights when you crave the down-home comfort of something richly flavored and satisfying. This dish can be on your dinner table within an hour but, like most tomato-flavored foods, it tastes even better the following day when flavors blend and mellow.

2 tablespoons olive oil
1 medium onion, diced
½ cup chopped celery
2 medium carrots, diced
2 medium fennel bulbs, quartered lengthwise and sliced
6 cups vegetable stock (see page 20)
1 (28-oz) can diced tomatoes
2 teaspoons salt
1 teaspoon freshly ground black pepper
Croutons for garnish (optional)

1. Heat olive oil in a soup pot, add onions and celery, and sauté until onions are translucent.
2. Add carrots and fennel, and sauté until vegetables are tender, about 5 minutes.
3. Add stock, tomatoes, salt and pepper. Cook over low heat for about 30 minutes.
4. Ladle into bowls and garnish with croutons.

Makes 8 servings.

Each serving contains about: 100 calories, 3g protein, 14g carbohydrate, 3g fiber, 5g fat, 3mg cholesterol, 663mg sodium.

Fennel Fettuccine

The Italians love fennel, and when you bring this fettuccine dish to the table you can say "buon appetito." Serve with glasses of red wine and hot crusty bread.

2 lbs fresh tomatoes, cored, seeded and quartered
12 green olives, pitted and chopped
¼ cup white wine
1 teaspoon oregano
1 teaspoon basil
4 tablespoons olive oil (divided)
2 fennel bulbs, quartered lengthwise and sliced (about 2 cups)
3 garlic cloves, minced
1 lb fettuccine pasta
¼ cup grated Parmesan cheese

1. Mix tomatoes, olives, white wine, oregano, basil and 1 tablespoon olive oil, and set aside to marinate 20 to 30 minutes.
2. Heat remaining olive oil in a medium pan, add fennel and garlic, and sauté until fennel is tender, about 6 minutes.
3. Add tomato mixture and heat a few minutes.
4. Cook fettuccine according to package directions.
5. Place the cooked pasta on a serving platter, top with fennel mixture and sprinkle with grated Parmesan.

Makes 4 servings.

Each serving contains about: 652 calories, 20g protein, 98g carbohydrate, 9g fiber, 19g fat, 5mg cholesterol, 472mg sodium.

Fennel, Mushroom and Olive Pizza

Pizza is everyone's favorite for an impromptu casual party. This one is easy, using canned pizza dough (in the refrigerated section of supermarkets) and canned pizza or spaghetti sauce.

1 medium fennel bulb, quartered lengthwise and thinly sliced
½ lb fresh mushrooms, washed and sliced
1 tablespoon olive oil
1 (10-oz) tube pizza dough
1 (10-oz) can prepared pizza sauce
4 oz mozzarella cheese, grated
4 tablespoons Parmesan cheese, grated
1 teaspoon garlic powder
1 teaspoon dried oregano
1 (6-oz) can black olives

1. Preheat oven to 450 degrees F, and lightly coat a 15 x 10-inch pizza pan with nonstick cooking spray.
2. Sauté fennel and mushrooms in olive oil for about 4 to 5 minutes, until fennel is tender. Set aside.
3. Follow instructions on pizza dough package.
4. After pizza is on pan, spread with sauce.
5. Sprinkle on both cheeses, garlic powder and oregano.
6. Top with fennel and mushrooms. Halve each olive and sprinkle on pizza.
7. Bake at 450 degrees F for about 8 to 10 minutes.

Makes one 15 x 10-inch pizza, about 4 servings.

Each serving contains about: 430 calories, 19g protein, 49g carbohydrate, 4g fiber, 18g fat, 21mg cholesterol, 1282mg sodium.

Grilled Fennel with Eggplant and Red Peppers

This is a wonderful side dish for summertime cooking on the barbecue grill. Make it even more colorful by adding green or yellow peppers.

6 small fennel bulbs (about 2 lbs)
3 red bell peppers (or green and yellow), seeded and cut lengthwise into quarters
3 small Japanese eggplants (about 1 lb), sliced in half lengthwise
¼ cup olive oil
1 to 1½ teaspoons dried oregano

1. Trim fennel at the root and remove the stalks down to the bulb. Blanch bulbs for about 10 minutes in boiling water. Drain. Cut bulbs lengthwise, then into ½-inch thick slices.
2. Brush fennel, peppers and eggplant with olive oil and oregano.
3. Place on grill and drizzle with more olive oil if necessary.
4. Grill until vegetables are fork tender.

Makes 6 servings.

Each serving contains about: 133 calories, 3g protein, 12g carbohydrate, 5g fiber, 9g fat, 0mg cholesterol, 140mg sodium.

G

Garlic
(Allium sativum)

History and lore: The word *garlic* or *garleac* comes from the Anglo-Saxon for "spear plant," because the growing bulb sends up erect branchless shoots.

According to a Turkish legend, when Satan was cast out of heaven "garlic sprouted where he first placed his left foot, and onions where he put his right." However, garlic truly originated in Central Asia, with the first written record appearing in Sanskrit writings about 5000 B.C. It was brought to the Middle East and Europe by trade and cultivation. The ancient Egyptians had a great love of the pungent bulb, and pyramid builders insisted that garlic should be included in their daily food rations. Several cloves of garlic were discovered in Tutankhamen's tomb, probably as a talisman to ward off evil spirits and disease in the After Life. Garlic was planted in the gardens of the King of Babylon, and praised in the writings of Homer.

Much superstition surrounds the garlic bulb. Ancient Greek and Roman warriors and gladiators took garlic prior to battle to ensure strength and courage, necklaces of garlic cloves were said to ward off personal devils, and garlic rubbed on doorknobs and window-frames discouraged vampires. Some believed that a garlic head hung on the bed-post would guarantee the birth of a baby boy; while Thomas Nashe, a 16th century writer, proclaimed *"Garlick hath properties that make a man winke, drinke and stinke."*

Garlic is famous in folk medicine for having miraculous properties and soothing many ailments: warding off hay fever, curing frostbite, epilepsy, backache, ulcers, dog bites, insect bites and scorpion stings. Recent medical studies have shown that garlic is helpful in reducing blood pressure, lowering cholesterol and protecting against cancer and diabetes.

Seasons when available: Year-round. When U.S.-grown garlic is out of season, produce markets will have bulbs from Mexico or the Southern Hemisphere (Argentina, Chile).

What to look for when shopping: Buy firm dry bulbs, with no soft spongy or withered areas, and no discolored, stained or sooty spots.

Good supermarkets will stock different varieties: Italian has the strongest flavor. The heads are small and the papery skin is pinkish in color. Creole is milder-flavored; heads are larger and the skin is white. The huge Elephant garlic (also known as Great-headed, Oriental or Tahiti garlic) is the mildest and sweetest, causing no strong garlic breath after eating it; individual cloves are dark pinkish.

Nutritional highlights: A source of calcium and sodium.

Amount for 4 servings: One bulb, containing a cluster of "cloves."

How to store: Always keep garlic bulbs dry. Keep them in a well-ventilated cool, dark area, in a paper sack — not plastic which will turn bulbs brown. Many kitchen supply stores sell garlic "cellars," usually pottery jars with perforations.

Another method: store peeled garlic cloves covered with olive oil in a screw-top glass jar in the refrigerator, for up to three months.

Basic prep: Peel away the thin papery skin covering the head; then peel skin off each clove. To remove clove skin easily, place it on cutting board and whack with the flat side of a wide knife; pull broken skin away. Slice clove into pieces, then chop finely. Crushing, mincing or finely chopping garlic releases wonderful pungent juices, making it more potent than when halved, sliced or left whole.

If left raw, garlic is pungent, assertive and robust. When lightly cooked, it becomes mellow and sweet. When cooked longer and slower, and allowed to caramelize, the flavor becomes more delicate, nutty and rich, but over-browning will turn it bitter.

Ways to serve: Thinly sliced raw Elephant garlic is superb on sandwiches with mayonnaise, lettuce and tomato. Chop garlic and add to stuffings, pastas and sauces; make your own garlicky croutons or garlic game chips. Roast whole garlic bulbs (mild-flavored Elephant garlic is best) and spread the delicious softened center on crusty French bread, thin toast or ¼-inch slices of jicama, or add to whipped potatoes.

Macho Garlic Nachos

This dish, which makes a great appetizer, is not for the faint-hearted; add more garlic to step up the voltage. If you like spicier nachos, use jalapeño-flavored Jack cheese.

> 3 large garlic bulbs, peeled and separated into cloves
> 1½ tablespoons cooking oil
> 1 (8-oz) bag unflavored tortilla chips
> ⅓ red onion, chopped
> 1 (4-oz) can chopped green Ortega chilies
> ½ cup pimiento-stuffed olives, sliced
> 2 cups grated Monterey Jack cheese
> ½ cup chopped cilantro

1. Toss the garlic cloves with oil, and bake at 300 degrees F for about 30 minutes or until soft.
2. Coat a 13 x 9 x 2-inch pan with nonstick cooking spray and spread bottom with tortilla chips.
3. Spread garlic, onion, chilies and olives evenly over the chips. Top with cheese.
4. Bake at 400 degrees F for about 5 minutes or until cheese melts.
5. Remove from oven and sprinkle with chopped cilantro.

Makes 4 servings.

Each serving contains about: 387 calories, 12g protein, 28g carbohydrate, 2g fiber, 26g fat, 34mg cholesterol, 698mg sodium.

Cheese-Stuffed Elephant Garlic

While these appetizers are baking, the savory aroma of fresh garlic fills the house and yet the flavor is surprisingly mild and sweet. Serve them as a light lunch accompanied by a salad, with crackers or hot French bread.

3 oz chive-flavored cream cheese
4 oz Stilton cheese
16 large Elephant garlic cloves, peeled
1 tablespoon olive oil

1. Mix together both cheeses until soft.
2. Scoop out a small hole in each garlic clove and fill with cheese mixture.
3. Place garlic in a shallow baking dish and drizzle with olive oil.
4. Bake at 350 degrees F for 20 minutes or until golden brown.
5. Arrange four garlic cloves on each plate.

Makes 4 servings.

Each serving contains about: 254 calories, 9g protein, 9g carbohydrate, 1g fiber, 20g fat, 49mg cholesterol, 221mg sodium.

Garlic Custards

We tend to think of custards as sweet dishes, but this one makes a lovely main dish along with a hearty soup, salad and good crusty bread.

    10 garlic cloves, medium to large size
    ½ cup chopped onion
    1 tablespoon olive oil
    ½ cup milk plus 2 tablespoons
    2 large eggs
    1 cup whipping cream
    ½ teaspoon dried thyme

1. Peel garlic, cut in half and place in pan. Cover with water and boil. Cook about 2 minutes. Drain well.
2. Sauté onion in olive oil until translucent.
3. In food processor or blender, purée garlic with milk, and blend till smooth. Whisk in eggs, cream, thyme and onions.
4. Divide into custard cups. Place in large baking pan with enough water to come about halfway up the sides of cups.
5. Bake at 325 degrees F for about 35 minutes or until custards are set. Serve warm.

Makes 6 servings.

Each serving contains about: 189 calories, 4g protein, 5g carbohydrate, 1g fiber, 17g fat, 118mg cholesterol, 48mg sodium.

Ginger

(Zingiber officinale)

Also known as: Green ginger; Gray ginger.

History and lore: The word ginger is derived from the Sanskrit *sringavera* which translates as "shaped like deer antlers," referring to the gnarled knobby appearance of the rhizome.

Born in the tropics, ginger is native to southern Asia and India — as old as the recorded history of humans. The people of China and India have used and valued ginger from ancient times, and have introduced it wherever they traded or settled. First century A.D. traders took ginger to Mediterranean countries; and by the 11th century its popularity had swept across Europe. It is mentioned in the Jewish Talmud and by Marco Polo. When ginger reached ancient Rome, officials slapped a high import tax on it so that the price in the market-place was ten times that of black pepper. The Spaniards took ginger to the West Indies and to Mexico soon after the Conquest, and by 1547 the spice was being sent back from Santiago, Chile to Spain.

The Chinese have always regarded fresh ginger not just as fine seasoning but also as potent medicine for a long list of disorders: an aid to digestion, treating colic and flatulence and restoring appetite; a prescription for colds, coughs, flu, scurvy and hangovers; and a restorative of men's sexual prowess. An ancient remedy for headache instructed sufferers to roast the root over an open fire then apply slices to the temples and forehead. The ancient Chinese believed a bite of ginger a day kept the doctor away, and about half of all Oriental herbal medicine still includes ginger root. Chinese travelers would munch on salty, spiced strips of preserved ginger to soothe them on cross-country journeys, and commercial fisherman would chew on a slug of ginger root to ward off bouts of seasickness. (A recent study by Brigham Young University and Mount Union College in Ohio has found powdered ginger root more effective than the anti-nausea drug Dramamine in blocking motion sickness.)

Seasons when available: You can buy fresh mature ginger root all year in supermarkets. Baby ginger is available from early summer to early autumn in Asian markets; they may also stock dried ginger root for brewing into a tea.

What to look for when shopping: The gnarled root should have a light brown, smooth skin with a slight sheen. Young shoots are succulent and milder-flavored; older roots are fibrous and have more bite and snap. Choose the hardest specimens you can find, with no wrinkles or signs of mold that indicate age. Inside flesh will be white.

Nutritional highlights: Vitamins A and C, and potassium.

Amount for 4 servings: Usually sold in 4-oz pieces.

How to store: Ginger likes to be *kept dry*. It keeps 2 to 3 weeks in the refrigerator, wrapped in paper towel (to absorb moisture that might produce mold) and sealed in a plastic bag. You can freeze ginger for about one month in foil or plastic wrap, but the texture will not be as firm after freezing and thawing. Or keep pieces of ginger immersed in dry Sherry in a covered jar in the refrigerator. In each case, slice off what you need and return the rest to storage where the cut will "heal."

Basic prep: Young ginger root need not be peeled, only washed. The skin is thin and translucent, and can be removed with a vegetable peeler. Mince ginger with a very fine grater, or run it through a food processor.

Ways to serve: The flavor of fresh ginger is peppery and pungent, giving a definite burst of flavor to heat up stir-fries and curries, and with a special affinity for garlic, cilantro and chilies. At the same time it has aromatic floral undertones that accent the sweetness of fruit, and make it a lovely addition to cakes, breads, ice cream and spiced teas.

Ginger's complex flavors blend well with the simple flavors relished in hot climates: ginger with dried legumes (central to India's vegetarian cuisines) and with almost every fruit and vegetable on Earth.

Sauté about 2 teaspoons ginger in a little butter, then add to cooked black beans, carrots, sweet potatoes or turnips. Or simmer ginger in a pan with sliced pears or pineapple.

Grind your own ultra-fresh spice: dry thin peeled slices of mature ginger in the sun then whirl them in a blender. You'll never go back to ordinary supermarket packs of ready-ground ginger.

Ginger Pear Soup

This soup is very gingery, and because the spice has subtle fruity undertones, it teams well with the flavors of lemon and pear. This soup is good served either hot or well chilled.

4 tablespoons butter or margarine
1½ tablespoons grated fresh ginger
2 lbs pears
Juice of 1 medium lemon
3 cups water
Salt and pepper to taste

1. Melt butter in soup pot, add grated ginger and cook gently over low heat for about 4 minutes.
2. Cut pears in quarters, remove cores and chop fruit.
3. Add pears, lemon juice and water to soup pot and simmer 20 to 30 minutes till pears are tender.
4. Put the mixture in a food processor or blender, and whirl until smooth. Add seasonings to taste.
5. Reheat soup if served hot, adding more water if too thick. If served cold, chill at least an hour.

Makes 4 servings.

Each serving contains about: 245 calories, 1g protein, 37g carbohydrate, 6g fiber, 12g fat, 31mg cholesterol, 256mg sodium.

Quinoa with Ginger

Quinoa is a healthful high-protein grain native to South America. This main dish has plenty of spices, but the fresh ginger is the one you'll remember.

2 tablespoons cooking oil
2 cups quinoa (sold in health-food stores or specialty markets)
2 teaspoons fresh ginger, peeled and minced
1 garlic clove, minced
1 teaspoon ground cinnamon
1 teaspoon ground turmeric
4 cups boiling water
1 cup *each* cut green beans, diced carrots, diced potatoes, broccoli and cauliflowerets
½ cup garden peas
1 tablespoon butter or margarine
1 medium onion, sliced
3 tablespoons cashew pieces

1. Heat oil in a soup pot. Add quinoa and stir briefly.
2. Add ginger, garlic, cinnamon and turmeric, and sauté for about 2 minutes.
3. Add water and let boil. Add all vegetables except the onion. Cover, and cook over low heat for about 30 minutes.
4. In a small pan, sauté onion in butter until golden; add cashews and stir until lightly toasted.
5. Transfer the quinoa-vegetable mixture to a serving dish and top with onions and cashews.

Makes 6 servings.

Each serving contains about: 346 calories, 12g protein, 51g carbohydrate, 9g fiber, 12g fat, 5mg cholesterol, 47mg sodium.

Gingered Papayas

The combination of fresh ginger and papaya makes this dessert wonderfully refreshing.

>   2 medium to large papayas, ripe but firm
>   2 tablespoons butter or margarine
>   2 tablespoons freshly squeezed lime juice
>   2 (¼-inch) slices ginger root, peeled and minced (about 1 tablespoon)
>   ¼ cup chopped walnuts

1. Cut papayas lengthwise and scoop out seeds.
2. Lightly coat a baking dish with nonstick cooking spray, and arrange fruit halves in dish.
3. Melt butter with lime juice and ginger, and spoon mixture into the cavity of each papaya.
4. Bake at 350 degrees F for 30 minutes, basting occasionally.
5. Sprinkle each papaya with chopped walnuts, and serve hot.

Makes 4 servings.

Each serving contains about: 161 calories, 2g protein, 17g carbohydrate, 3g fiber, 11g fat, 15mg cholesterol, 64mg sodium.

Ginger Pound Cake with Apricot-Orange Sauce

The smell of fresh ginger baking in this lovely cake permeates the house with a wonderful fragrance. Other toppings such as raspberry or even chocolate make a luscious finish, but liqueur-spiked apricot is especially delectable.

2 cups unbleached all-purpose flour
½ teaspoon baking powder
1 cup (2 sticks) butter or margarine
1¼ cups granulated sugar
3 large eggs
2 tablespoons fresh grated ginger
½ cup milk
Apricot-Orange Sauce (see recipe below)

1. Coat a 9 x 5-inch loaf pan with nonstick cooking spray, or grease lightly. Preheat oven to 300 degrees F.
2. Sift flour with baking powder.
3. In a separate bowl, cream butter with sugar and beat till fluffy. Add eggs one at a time, mixing well. Mix in fresh ginger.
4. Add flour alternating with the milk, beating on low speed until well mixed.
5. Pour into prepared loaf pan and bake at 300 degrees F for 1¾ to 2 hours, until knife inserted in center comes out clean. Cool on a wire rack.
6. Cut cake into neat slices and drizzle each slice with Apricot-Orange sauce.

Apricot-Orange Sauce (makes 1 cup)

½ cup apricot jam or preserves
¼ cup freshly squeezed orange juice
2 tablespoons orange liqueur (Triple Sec or Grand Marnier)

Heat apricot jam and orange juice together over low heat, stirring until smooth.
Remove from heat and add liqueur. Allow to cool.

Makes one 9 x 5-inch cake, about 16 slices.

Each slice (with sauce) contains about: 271 calories, 3g protein, 36g carbohydrate, 1g fiber, 13g fat, 72mg cholesterol, 145mg sodium.

Gobo root

(Arctium lappa)

Also known as: Burdock; Great burdock; Beggar's button.

History and lore: Native to northern China and Siberia, gobo is cultivated in Japan where it has been an important vegetable since about the 10th century. It's considered a delicacy in Southeast Asia.

The root was valued by ancient folk healers as a blood purifier and strengthener, a tonic after sickness, a relief medicine for arthritis and skin diseases.

In modern-day Tokyo, gobo soup has its advocates. Sales are booming of a canned vegetable stock made with gobo, radishes, carrots and dried mushrooms, said to prevent cancer, cure diabetes, lower blood pressure and banish hangovers. The health-conscious and the stressed are buying up the soup by the case, and suppliers say they are hard-pressed to keep up with demand. Even the prime minister swears by it, and it has become the talk of Japan. Why is gobo considered so healthful? If the Japanese think it's a wonder root, should Americans be eating more of it?

Seasons when available: Year-round, in Oriental markets, natural-food stores, and supermarkets selling to Japanese and Taiwanese customers.

What to look for when shopping: Look for firm unbroken roots with taut skin, avoiding any that are limp and floppy, or with dry wrinkled skin. Gobo has a slender shape, up to two feet long and no thicker than a medium carrot. Thicker roots can be stringy. Peel is dark-brown or rusty-beige, and flesh is grayish-white with a tender-crisp texture. The earthy flavor is similar to artichoke hearts or salsify.

Nutritional highlights: Low in calories, high in fiber and potassium; modest source of iron and calcium.

Amount for 4 servings: One medium root (about 4 oz), when used as a flavoring in soups, risottos, etc.

How to store: Wrap in damp paper towel, then a plastic bag, and store in refrigerator for a few days. For longer storage, refrigerate in a dish of water.

Basic prep: Scrub the root thoroughly with a stiff vegetable brush to remove any mud and tiny rootlets. Don't remove the thin peel as it contains much of the flavor and nutrition. To avoid discoloration (and eliminate the slightly bitter flavor) soak sliced gobo in cold acidulated water for 15 minutes before use.

Gobo is a tough fibrous root so it must be shredded or sliced thinly or it will not become tender. When cooking with other vegetables, add gobo first and cook till almost tender before adding other ingredients. Gobo chunks can be tenderized by combining with 2 cups water and ½ teaspoon baking soda; bring to boiling then drain and rinse, before adding to soups or stews.

Ways to serve: Sauté gobo alone or with other vegetables; stir fry; deep fry in a tempura batter; simmer in a well-seasoned broth; serve hot with a soy dipping sauce; add shredded gobo to a risotto of brown rice, shredded carrots and Oriental mushrooms.

Gobo and Guacamole

Offer this appetizer at your next party. The crispness of young gobo makes a welcome change from corn chips, and its distinct flavor counterbalances the smooth texture of the guacamole dip.

> 1 to 1½ lb gobo root (about 6 or 7)
> 1 ripe avocado, peeled and pitted
> 2 tablespoons mayonnaise
> 1 tablespoon *each* cooking oil, lemon juice and instant minced onion
> 1 teaspoon seasoned salt
> 1 medium tomato, cut in small wedges (optional garnish)

1. If gobo skin is thin, do not peel. Cut the gobo into thin dipping sticks. Plunge pieces into a bowl of acidulated water (1 tablespoon lemon juice to 1 cup), to avoid discoloration while making dip.
2. Put avocado, mayonnaise, oil, lemon juice, instant onion and salt in food processor, and purée.
3. Put dip in serving bowl, and garnish with tomato wedges.
4. Serve chilled, surrounded by drained gobo dipping sticks.

Makes 1 cup of dip and 2½ to 3 cups of dipping sticks, about 4 servings.

Each serving contains about: 246 calories, 3g protein, 25g carbohydrate, 7g fiber, 17g fat, 4mg cholesterol, 583mg sodium.

Gobo Root Soup with Egg Drop

Shiitake mushrooms and Oriental seasonings bring out the flavor of the gobo, a popular root in Japanese cuisine. Sesame oil and oyster sauce are sold in ethnic sections of supermarkets and Oriental markets.

6 shiitake mushrooms, sliced
2 teaspoons light sesame oil
1 large gobo root, peeled and cut into slices
1 piece fresh ginger root, ¼-inch thick
1 large carrot, peeled and sliced
½ cup chopped onion
7 cups vegetable stock (see page 20), or vegetable bouillon (1 teaspoon
    or 1 cube for each cup water)
1 tablespoon soy sauce
1 tablespoon oyster sauce
2 scallions, sliced into ½-inch lengths
3 tablespoons chopped fresh parsley (or 1 tablespoon dried parsley)
1 large egg, beaten

1. Soak mushrooms in lukewarm water for 30 minutes. When soft, remove stems. Drain and set aside.
2. Heat oil and sauté gobo, ginger, carrot and onion for about 5 minutes. Add drained mushrooms and sauté 2 more minutes. Add 2 tablespoons water and continue cooking 2 minutes. Discard ginger root.
3. In soup pot bring vegetable stock to a boil, and add vegetables. Simmer till gobo is just tender. Add soy sauce, oyster sauce, scallions and parsley, and bring back to a boil.
4. Pour beaten egg in slowly, stirring constantly until it separates into shreds. Remove from heat, and serve.

Makes 4 servings.

Each serving contains about: 151 calories, 5g protein, 23g carbohydrate, 4g fiber, 7g fat, 61mg cholesterol, 378mg sodium.

Japanese Gobo Stir-fry

This recipe is spicy. If you prefer a milder dish, reduce or eliminate the red-pepper flakes. Mirin, sesame or peanut oil are sold in Oriental grocers or Oriental sections of supermarkets.

5 medium gobo roots
1 tablespoon soy sauce
1 tablespoon mirin
2 teaspoons mild honey
1 tablespoon sesame or peanut oil
1 medium carrot, cut into matchstick-size pieces
¼ cup chopped scallions
½ teaspoon hot red-pepper flakes

1. Peel gobo and cut into matchstick-size pieces. Place in cold water to prevent discoloration; set aside.
2. In a small bowl, mix soy sauce, mirin and honey; set aside.
3. Heat oil in a wok or fry pan. Drain and blot gobo. When oil is hot, stir-fry gobo, carrots and scallions for 2 to 3 minutes, until gobo is no longer raw.
4. Sprinkle with red-pepper flakes and stir for another minute. Add soy-sauce mixture and sauté until liquid is gone, about 1 minute.
5. Serve at room temperature.

Makes 4 servings.

Each serving contains about: 137 calories, 2g protein, 25g carbohydrate, 3g fiber, 4g fat, 0mg cholesterol, 270mg sodium.

H

Horseradish

(Cultivated: *Armoracia rusticana*, or wild: *A. lapathifolia*)

History and lore: This heavy long taproot with the powerful flavor probably originated in central and eastern Europe and western Asia, and cultivation spread it northward to Scandinavia and westward to England in Renaissance times. It now grows wild throughout Europe and North America.

Cultivated in many states of the United States, much of it is processed with vinegar to make bottled horseradish sauce or zesty cocktail sauce for seafood. However, fresh horseradish roots are a fairly recent addition to U.S. produce markets because they have gained the attention of trendy chefs. Compared to the bottled variety, the freshly grated root is potent stuff, not for the timid — it's wonderful for clearing the sinuses!

Centuries ago, horseradish was gathered in the wild and used to alleviate congestion from colds, to relieve stomach problems such as colic and worms, and as a tonic to restore the appetite.

Each country has its own way with horseradish: most enthusiastic are Germans, Finns, Norwegians, Danes, British, Russians and Hungarians. The English have it on their roast beef, the Poles with veal, the Hungarians with pork sausages, and Japanese serve their *wasabi* variety in a soy-seasoned dip for seafood and raw sushi. In southern Germany the word for "horseradish" is *Kren*, and at the *Viktualienmarkt* in Munich you can still occasionally see *Krenweiberl* ("little horseradish women") in folkloric dress selling big baskets of fresh *Kren* that they have grown.

East European Jewish families (and U.S. Jews from that part of the world) like horseradish with gefilte fish at the Passover seder. The pungent bitterness that brings tears to the eyes is a reminder of sorrowful years in slavery centuries ago. You can go to pickle stores in New York's old Jewish quarter and watch while fresh horseradish is finely shredded in a hand-cranked grater, in traditions that stretch back to Jewish culture in the Old World.

Seasons when available: Year-round but especially late fall to early spring.

What to look for when shopping: The root is about 6 to 12 inches long and 1 to 3 inches thick, with several round knobs at one end; a pale brown wrinkled skin and white flesh. Avoid roots with sprouts or that have a greenish tinge. Choose roots that are firm, heavy and unblemished. The flavor will be pungent and hot, especially when very fresh; the heavier ones are supposed to have greater flavor. Horseradish has no odor until the tissues are broken, releasing the mustard oils that give its distinctive bite.

Wasabi (*Wasabia Japonica*), though unrelated to white horseradish, has a similar strong flavor, but wasabi is less sharp and more aromatic.

Nutritional highlights: Low in calories and sodium, high in vitamin C, calcium, iron and potassium.

Amount for 4 servings: The root is often sold in 3 to 4-oz cello bags.

How to store: Wrapped in plastic in the refrigerator, the roots will keep for about 3 weeks.

Basic prep: When preparing horseradish, be sure to wear rubber gloves and don't touch your eyes. Because fumes from the root can make your eyes tear, turn your head away from the chopping board, grater or food processor.

Immediately before using, scrub the root and remove peel with a sharp knife. If any soft spots or mold have developed, scrape them off before using. Grate the amount you need with a very sharp metal grater, or use a food processor.

Horseradish is generally eaten raw, in small amounts, but try cooking chunks in stews — the peppery bite is tempered to a milder sweetness similar to turnip.

Ways to serve: Grate fresh horseradish into hot cooked vegetables such as beans, beets, celery root, mashed potatoes or parsnips; into cream sauces, mayonnaise, sour cream; and into applesauce or cranberry sauce for a surprising zip.

Horseradish Sauce #1 (with scallions)

Horseradish makes fine condiments to accent other dishes such as baked pota-toes and steamed vegetables. Here are three sauces with different seasonings: as we can't decide which we prefer, we include all three to let the decision be yours.

    1 cup plain yogurt or dairy sour cream
    2 medium scallions, finely minced
    2 tablespoons freshly grated horseradish, or prepared horseradish
    4 tablespoons butter or margarine
    1 teaspoon tarragon vinegar

1. Combine all ingredients in a small saucepan over low heat.
2. Warm gently until butter is melted and the sauce is heated through.
3. Serve at room temperature.

Makes 1 cup.

Each tablespoon contains about: 35 calories, 1g protein, 1g carbohydrate, 0g fiber, 3g fat, 8mg cholesterol, 41mg sodium.

Horseradish Sauce #2 (with egg yolks)

You may want to reserve this richer sauce for an impressive accompaniment to dishes at dinner parties or other special occasions.

    1 small onion, minced
    2 tablespoons butter or margarine
    1 cup light cream
    2 egg yolks, slightly beaten
    ¼ cup freshly grated horseradish, or prepared horseradish
    ¼ teaspoon cayenne pepper

1. In a medium pan, sauté onion in butter until translucent.
2. Add cream and bring to boil.
3. Add beaten egg yolks and stir constantly until well blended. Add horseradish and cook gently until slightly thickened. Add cayenne pepper.
4. Serve warm.

Makes 1 cup.

Each tablespoon contains about: 67 calories, 1g protein, 1g carbohydrate, 0g fiber, 7g fat, 47mg cholesterol, 21mg sodium.

Horseradish Sauce #3 (cream style)

This sauce smooths and softens the lusty flavor of the horseradish by combining it with creamy cottage cheese, blending it into a velvety topping for steamed vegetables, baked potatoes, hot rice or noodles.

> 1 cup cottage cheese
> 2 tablespoons fresh grated horseradish
> 1 teaspoon white vinegar
> ¼ teaspoon freshly ground black pepper
> 2 tablespoons olive oil
> 3 tablespoons unbleached all-purpose flour
> 1½ cups milk

1. Combine cottage cheese, horseradish, vinegar and pepper in a food processor; purée and set aside.
2. In a small pan whisk together olive oil and flour until smooth, and cook over medium heat until bubbly, stirring constantly for about 3 to 5 minutes.
3. Add milk to pan and keep stirring until mixture is thick and boiling.
4. Stir in cottage cheese mixture. Heat through, but do not boil.

Makes 2½ cups sauce, about 6 servings.

Each serving contains about: 129 calories, 7g protein, 7g carbohydrate, 1g fiber, 8g fat, 13mg cholesterol, 172mg sodium.

Rosy Relish

This pretty beet relish, with plenty of zip, will keep well for up to three months in a tightly covered container in the refrigerator.

    4 oz fresh horseradish, peeled and diced
    1 (16-oz) can or jar beets, sliced or julienne-cut
    ¼ cup white vinegar
    1 tablespoon granulated sugar, or to taste
    1 teaspoon salt
    ½ teaspoon caraway seeds

1. In food processor fitted with a steel blade, whirl horseradish until finely grated.
2. Drain beets and add to processor with vinegar, sugar, salt and caraway seeds.
3. Turn processor on/off several times until beets are grated and mixture is blended.

Makes about 1½ cups, about 6 servings.

Each serving contains about: 50 calories, 1g protein, 12g carbohydrate, 2g fiber, 1g fat, 0mg cholesterol, 563mg sodium.

Cheese and Horseradish Spread

This easy spread can be prepared entirely in the microwave, so it goes together in a flash. Serve it on crackers or Melba toasts, as an appetizer or snack.

    ½ lb processed Cheddar cheese
    3 tablespoons commercial creamed horseradish
    ½ cup commercial mayonnaise
    2 teaspoons diced green chilies

1. Cube cheese and put in microwave dish. Heat on HIGH for 1 minute.
2. Blend in rest of ingredients. Cook on 60% power for about 10 minutes. Stir three times, every 3½ minutes, until melted and well-blended.

Makes 2 cups.

Each tablespoon contains about: 51 calories, 2g protein, 1g carbohydrate, 0g fiber, 5g fat, 9mg cholesterol, 124mg sodium.

J

Jerusalem artichoke

(Helianthus tuberosus)

Also known as: *Girasole*; *Girasol*; *Topinambour*; *Racine de tournesol*; and the brand names: "Sunchoke"; "Sun Root."

History and lore: They don't come from Jerusalem or the Holy Land, and are no relation to the artichoke. Jerusalem is said to be a corruption of the Spanish *girasole* or Italian *girasol*, "sunflower," and they are actually the root of one variety of the wild American sunflower. The name "Sunchoke" (from Frieda's Finest in Los Angeles) is used on the West Coast.

These roots originated in North America; Native Americans were roasting them long before the arrival of Columbus, and introduced them later to the colonists who considered them a mainstay in staving off famine during the "six weeks want" — the period between the end of winter food stores and the first harvests. Samuel de Champlain in 1605 found Indian tribes growing the vegetable on Cape Cod, and sent some of the tubers back to France, after which they were cultivated in Italy, Germany and England. They were labeled "artichokes" in 17th century Europe so that the familiar word would make them accepted by the peasants as good nourishing food.

Artichokes are often made into a delicious pasta that's safe for people allergic to wheat, and they are also recommended for diabetics: instead of starch, the roots contain a polysaccharide called *inulin*, which is slowly digested. The tubers can reduce blood sugar as well as levels of urea (a kidney waste-product). Food manufacturers produce levulose (D-fructose), a sweetener suitable for diabetics, from the inulin in sunchokes.

Artichokes do have a drawback: they create gas, especially if they are first-of-the-season, freshly harvested or bought young from a farmers' market. An early farmer, John Goodyer, declared in 1621: "*...whichwaysoever they be drest and eaten, they stir up and cause a filthie loathesome stinking winde within the bodie, thereby causing the belly to bee much pained...*". However, the modern-day remedies for this problem are simple: eat small portions to begin with; or cook chokes with the herb *epazote*; or use a few drops of Beano or Be Sure (directions on each package), if your digestion needs help.

Seasons when available: Generally October to April, although you may find a few on sale during the summer.

What to look for when shopping: Smooth skinned, firm roots, similar to fresh ginger or knobbly potatoes, with skin that ranges from light buff through yellowish, to brown, red and purple. Avoid any with soft spots, with sprouts or that look green. The inside flesh is white and crisp like water chestnuts; after cooking the flavor is nutty and somewhat like artichokes.

Nutritional highlights: A good source of iron and niacin. When first harvested, calories are low; calories rise (to about 75 per 3½ oz) after a few months' storage, as inulin is converted to simple sugars.

Amount for 4 servings: About 1 lb.

How to store: Chokes are thin-skinned and soon shrivel when exposed to dry air. Wrapped in plastic, in the refrigerator, they keep for about a week. Freezing will make them darken and mushy.

Basic prep: Rinse under cold water and scrub the roots well. Peel them or not, but the cut flesh oxydizes and darkens when exposed to air. To prevent discoloration, cover with cold water and a spoonful of lemon juice, or cook sliced chokes right away.

Ways to serve: Chokes can be eaten either raw or cooked. Serve them sliced or julienned in salads. Chop and add them to stir-fries, or bake them whole as a change from potatoes (at 350 degrees for between 35 and 60, depending on age of chokes). Steaming the roots takes only 10 or 15 minutes, depending on their size. Serve with butter, a squeeze of lemon juice or a dusting of nutmeg, according to taste.

Artichoke-Spinach Dip

Raw Jerusalem artichokes make delicious crudités, served well chilled with a carefully seasoned dip. This one makes a great party dish. Prepare the dip the previous day to let flavors blend and mellow.

 1 (10-oz) package frozen chopped spinach
 2 cups commercial low-calorie mayonnaise
 ½ cup chopped scallions
 ½ cup chopped parsley, stems removed
 Salt and pepper to taste
 1 lb Jerusalem artichokes

1. Put all ingredients except artichokes in a food processor or blender, and whirl until smooth. Set aside to let flavors blend.
2. Wash and peel artichokes. Cut into slices that are not too thin, but firm enough to scoop up the dip.
3. Place dip in center of serving bowl, surrounded by neatly arranged artichoke slices.

Makes about 3 cups dip, about 12 servings.

Each serving (including artichokes) contains about: 92 calories, 2g protein, 10g carbohydrate, 1g fiber, 5g fat, 20mg cholesterol, 115mg sodium.

Sunchoke Crème

This versatile dish can be served in various ways: as a starter to a meal, as a vegetable accompaniment to a main course, or as a dip.

4 tablespoons butter or margarine
⅓ cup water
1 medium russet potato, peeled and thinly sliced
½ cup grated onion
2 lbs Jerusalem artichokes, peeled and thinly sliced
½ cup light cream

1. Melt butter in water and add potato, onion and artichokes. Simmer until tender, about 12 to 15 minutes.
2. Put in food processor and whirl until well blended.
3. Return to pan and add cream slowly. Stir while heating gently, and serve warm.

Makes about 2½ cups, about 6 servings.

Each serving contains about: 265 calories, 4g protein, 33g carbohydrate, 3g fiber, 14g fat, 43mg cholesterol, 93mg sodium.

Stewed Chokes

As Jerusalem artichokes become more readily available in supermarkets, especially during winter months, this side dish will add a flavorful interest to meals for your family.

    1 large onion, chopped
    2 tablespoons butter or margarine
    1½ lbs Jerusalem artichokes, peeled and sliced medium thick
    2 garlic cloves, minced
    ¼ teaspoon dried thyme
    1½ cups vegetable stock (on page 20), or vegetable bouillon (1 teaspoon
        or 1 cube for each cup water)
    1 cup dry white wine
    2 teaspoons Worcestershire sauce

1. Sauté onion in butter until translucent.
2. Add artichokes, garlic and thyme, stirring a few minutes to blend.
3. Add stock, wine and Worcestershire sauce. Reduce heat and cook until artichokes are tender.

Makes 4 servings.

Each serving contains about: 249 calories, 4g protein, 36g carbohydrate, 3g fiber, 7g fat, 17mg cholesterol, 121mg sodium.

Jicama

(Pachyrhizus erosus and *P.tuberosus)*

Also known as: Mexican potato; Mexican turnip; Yam bean; Mexican yam bean; *Ahipa*; *Sicama* (Philippines); *Sa Gord* or *Saa Got* (China).

History and lore: *P.erosus* originated in Mexico, and *P.tuberosus* in the Amazon region of South America. Jicama (pronounced HEE-kah-mah) is the tuberous root of a leguminous vine, a member of the pea family, now cultivated in those areas and in China and India. In the 17th century Spaniards took jicama to the Philippines, and from there it spread to other Pacific islands and to Asia.

Seasons when available: Almost year-round in some markets. Many Latin, Chinese and specialty markets stock it from November to June.

What to look for when shopping: These tubers can be either round like beets, or long and slender like icicles, although the globular shape is more common in the U.S. The skin is brownish gray; inside flesh is white and crisp, with a mild sweet flavor similar to fresh waterchestnuts. *Jicama de aqua* varieties have clear juices; *jicama de leche* types have milky juice. Choose firm, unblemished roots. Size varies between 4 and 8 inches diameter. Some are sold whole; very large ones may be cut in halves or quarters, although bigger tubers tend to be woody and tough.

Nutritional highlights: Low in calories and sodium; a good source of calcium, potassium and vitamin C.

Amount for 4 servings: About ½ to 1 lb.

How to store: Keep dry in the vegetable drawer in the refrigerator. Once cut, wrap well in plastic and use within a week.

Basic prep: Whether serving it raw or cooked, you need to peel away the rough outer skin. After cutting, plunge into ice water until ready to use, to heighten crispness. Cut into sticks for appetizers: party-givers love jicama in trays of crudités because it doesn't discolor or wilt, no matter how many rounds of drinks are served. For a crisp addition to salads, shred, dice, julienne or cut into thin rounds. For quick stir-fries, slice thinly: the jicama won't soften, but will retain its crispness and underlying sweetness while absorbing pungent seasonings.

Ways to serve: Jicama can replace fresh water chestnuts in Chinese recipes. For a crunchy South-of-the-Border snack, cut peeled jicama into fingers, sprinkle with lime juice, then dust with salt and chili powder. Sweet tasting jicama blends beautifully in salads of orange slices, papaya chunks and sliced sweet onions with a little fresh chopped cilantro.

Tostada Salad Isadora

These vegetable tostadas are similar to those served at the famous Isadora Restaurant in Mexico City.

 1 cup peeled shredded jicama
 1 cup scraped and shredded carrots
 1 cup shredded Monterey Jack cheese
 1 dark-green Serrano chili pepper, seeded and minced
 ½ red bell pepper, cut into 1-inch long strips
 3 tablespoons chopped fresh cilantro
 3 tablespoons unseasoned rice vinegar
 ¼ cup olive oil
 ½ teaspoon salt
 4 tostada shells

1. In a medium-size bowl combine and toss all ingredients, except tostada shells.
2. Spoon mixture onto tostada shells, mounding it up in the center and leaving a ½-inch edge.
3. Serve at room temperature.

Makes 4 servings.

Each serving contains about: 323 calories, 9g protein, 16g carbohydrate, 2g fiber, 25g fat, 25mg cholesterol, 433mg sodium.

Jicama Salsa

Bland jicama makes a perfect companion to hot chilies. Serve this salsa either chilled or at room temperature, on baked potatoes or steamed vegetables.

½ small jicama, peeled
1 small onion
½ large green pepper, seeded
1 tablespoon lemon juice
½ cup chopped cilantro, stems removed
2 oz chopped canned green chilies
2 garlic cloves, peeled
1 large can (28-oz) diced tomatoes

1. Combine all ingredients except tomatoes in a food processor. Process in small batches to a chunky consistency.
2. Add diced tomatoes, and stir to mix.
3. Serve at room temperature or chill at least one hour.

Makes 4 cups, about 16 servings.

Each serving contains about: 17 calories, 1g protein, 4g carbohydrate, 1g fiber, 1g fat, 0mg cholesterol, 14mg sodium.

Mexicali Salad

This colorful refreshing salad, served on a bed of crisp romaine lettuce, adds good taste to any lunch or dinner.

½ lb (1 medium) jicama, peeled
3 tablespoons fresh orange juice
1 head romaine lettuce
4 scallions, peeled and sliced
1 ripe avocado, peeled and cut into 8 slices
1 orange, peeled and sectioned into 8 pieces
1 cup vinaigrette dressing

1. Slice jicama into matchstick pieces and marinate in orange juice for about 15 minutes.
2. When ready to assemble, line each plate with romaine lettuce.
3. Arrange scallions, avocado and orange sections around plates. Add marinated jicama.
4. Drizzle with vinaigrette dressing.

Makes 4 servings.

Each serving contains about: 425 calories, 4g protein, 17g carbohydrate, 8g fiber, 40g fat, 0mg cholesterol, 17mg sodium.

K

Kohlrabi

(*Brassica oleracea*, sub.sp. *gongylodes*)

Also known as: Cabbage turnip.

History and lore: The funny name "kohlrabi" comes via German from the Latin *caulis rapum* meaning "cabbage turnip," an apt description because although it looks like a turnip, it's a member of the *Brassica* family that includes cabbage, broccoli and cauliflower. Purists point out that it's not, strictly speaking, a root, but a thickened stem growing just above ground. In fact, Germans call it *Kohlrabi uber der Erde*, "above-ground kohlrabi" to distinguish it from *Kohlrabi unter der Erde*, "underground kohlrabi," the turnip-like rutabaga or Swede.

The vegetable is a native of Northern Europe, and was first described in the 16th century, but didn't enter the English language nor was it known in the United States until the 19th century. However twelve centuries ago, Charlemagne the Great, that medieval promoter of agriculture, ordered that kohlrabi be planted throughout his empire, which stretched from the Ebro River in Spain to the Elbe River in Germany.

Shoppers in produce sections of U.S. supermarkets may still look on kohlrabi as a strange curiosity, but the people of Germany, Austria, northern France, Hungary and Russia, have no hesitation about including kohlrabi in many dishes.

Seasons when available: Year-round, although supplies may be more plentiful in late spring. If not stocked by supermarkets, check local farmers' markets.

What to look for when shopping: A globular swollen stem, green or purple in color, from which leaves sprout. Choose small or medium size, about 2 to 2½ inches in diameter, with firm smooth skins. Flavor is turnip-like but sweeter, with a juicy crisp texture; larger ones lack flavor but can hold savory stuffings. The leaves, which should be stored and cooked separately, should look young and green (not yellowed); their flavor is similar to collards or kale.

Nutritional highlights: Low in calories and sodium; high in potassium; a good source of vitamins A and C and calcium.

Amount for 4 servings: About 1½ lb, four medium size.

How to store: Wrapped in plastic and refrigerated, the stem will keep for up to one week. Leaves should be separately bagged and refrigerated, and used promptly after purchase.

Basic prep: Trim and peel away all woody portions. Raw kohlrabi is not recommended as the flesh can be unpleasantly bitter and tough, but careful cooking produces a sweet delicacy. Kohlrabi leaves are cooked like spinach. The stem can be steamed, boiled or baked. Cook slices as you would turnips in lightly salted boiling water in a heavy pan for 15 to 20 minutes.

Ways to serve: Serve hot, simply seasoned with butter, salt and pepper, or in a cream sauce, or an onion-parsley sauce. Or shred the stem and cook in a vegetable broth or add to soups and stews. Or sauté in olive oil or butter, and chill to serve as a salad with fresh herbs.

Kohlrabi in Cream Sauce

This recipe was inspired by one from Germany, where kohlrabi is immensely popular. The smooth velvety sauce makes a delectable accompaniment for this unusual vegetable, fit for an epicure.

3 lbs kohlrabi
2½ cups vegetable stock (see page 20) (divided)
7 tablespoons butter or margarine
7 tablespoons unbleached all-purpose flour
1 cup milk
½ cup whipping cream
½ cup chopped parsley for topping

1. Peel and slice kohlrabi. Cover with about 1½ cups stock in a medium pan. Cook until tender, about 20 minutes. Drain and reserve liquid.
2. Melt butter and stir in flour. Add milk and rest of stock. Heat until barely boiling. Reduce heat and blend in whipping cream.
3. Add kohlrabi and reheat. Top with chopped parsley.

Makes 6 servings.

Each serving contains about: 310 calories, 7g protein, 26g carbohydrate, 4g fiber, 22g fat, 66mg cholesterol, 233mg sodium.

Stuffed Kohlrabi

When kohlrabi is stuffed, it makes a superb main dish, served with a fresh green salad and a fruit dessert.

4 medium kohlrabi
2 cups seasoned bread crumbs
5 scallions, peeled and finely chopped
1 large egg, well beaten
¼ cup sour cream
2 teaspoons garlic powder
2 tablespoons butter or margarine, melted

1. Boil kohlrabi in water to cover for about 30 minutes or until tender.
2. In a bowl mix all other ingredients.
3. Hollow out center of each kohlrabi from the stem end, leaving a shell.
4. Mash kohlrabi centers and mix with bread-crumb mixture. If too dry, add more melted butter.
5. Fill kohlrabi shells with bread-crumb mixture, and arrange in a baking dish.
6. Bake at 350 degrees F for 20 minutes.

Makes 4 servings.

Each serving contains about: 357 calories, 12g protein, 51g carbohydrate, 5g fiber, 13g fat, 77mg cholesterol, 556mg sodium.

Winter Root Risotto

This hearty rice casserole, with its medley of roots, is delicately tinted and scented with saffron. Serve it with crisp greens and chilled glasses of dry white wine.

1 cup diced kohlrabi
½ cup *each* diced carrot and diced parsnip
2 garlic cloves, minced
4 tablespoons butter or margarine (divided)
½ teaspoon *each* dried thyme and granulated sugar
Salt and pepper to taste
2 tablespoons olive oil
1 cup chopped onion
¼ teaspoon crumbled saffron threads
1½ cups raw long-grain rice
4 cups mock-chicken broth (divided)
½ cup freshly grated Parmesan cheese
¼ cup chopped fresh parsley leaves

1. In a large skillet, sauté and stir kohlrabi, carrot, parsnip and garlic in 2 tablespoons of the butter over moderate heat for about 5 minutes.
2. Add thyme, sugar, salt and pepper to taste, and cook covered until vegetables are tender, about 15 minutes. Transfer vegetables to a bowl, cover and set aside.
3. Add oil and remaining 2 tablespoons butter to pan and cook onion and saffron over moderate heat, stirring occasionally, until onion is golden, about 15 minutes.
4. Mix in rice and cook, stirring constantly, until rice turns translucent. Stir in 2½ cups of the broth and simmer until most of broth is absorbed. Add about 1 cup of remaining broth and cook 15 minutes.
5. Stir in vegetables and cook until rice is tender, about 5 minutes.
6. Remove pan from heat and stir in cheese, parsley and remaining broth.

Makes 6 servings.

Each serving contains about: 358 calories, 9g protein, 45g carbohydrate, 2g fiber, 16g fat, 28mg cholesterol, 995mg sodium.

Kohlrabi and Persimmon Purée

Brilliantly colored persimmons make a dazzling presentation on the dinner table. Use Japanese (Hachiya) persimmons as they do not have to be as soft as other varieties, and the shells hold their shape. Serve as a sweet side-dish, or a lovely dessert topped with a puff of whipped cream.

> 2 kohlrabi, peeled and quartered
> 4 persimmons
> 2 tablespoons orange liqueur (for instance, Grand Marnier, Triple Sec)
> 3 tablespoons mild honey
> Whipped cream (optional)

1. Boil kohlrabi in water to cover, for 10 to 15 minutes or until tender. Drain.
2. Remove tops of persimmons, about 1 inch from top. Scoop out persimmon flesh and place in a food processor bowl with kohlrabi, liqueur and honey; purée.
3. Fill persimmon shells with purée, and chill.
4. When ready to serve as a dessert, top each shell with a small dab of whipped cream, if desired.

Makes 4 servings.

Each serving contains about: 274 calories, 7g protein, 68g carbohydrate, 8g fiber, 1g fat, 0mg cholesterol, 71mg sodium.

L

Leek

(Allium ampeloprasum or *A.porrum)*

Also known as: Flag onion; Poor man's asparagus.

History and lore: Is the leek a root? No, not really. Like kohlrabi, the main part of a leek consists of fleshy leaf bases; however in culinary use it is often grouped with onions, scallions and garlic, and treated like a root.

Where did it originate? The debate continues: Some say in Asia or the Mediterranean, but Northern Europe is most likely. Whatever the case, ancient Egyptians not only cultivated leeks, they worshipped them. Juvenal wrote that Egypt was a country where "onions are adored and leeks are gods." Pliny declared that the finest leeks came from Egypt; and the Israelites, after they had fled that country, sadly lamented about the leeks they had left behind them.

Leeks have a long history in the British Isles and, according to Chaucer, they were "wel loved" in his time. Each participant at medieval spring plowing festivals had to contribute a leek to the communal stew served after the competitions. Even today, the cult of the leek is still celebrated at the village of Ashington in the county of Northumberland (which claims to be "the leek capital of the world"); rivalry is intense as the people grow leeks of tremendous size, and the Leek Show each September ends with a great boil up of the prize-winning vegetables into a soup for all.

The Welsh are particularly fond of the leek and consider it their national emblem. They wear bits of the vegetable in their lapel buttonholes on St. David's Day, in memory of the victory of King Cadwallader over the Saxons in A.D. 640. During that ancient battle, the Welsh soldiers had worn leeks on their helmets as identification badges — so they wouldn't slay their own men by mistake!

Seasons when available: All year, with the peak from October through May.

What to look for when shopping: Shaped like giant green onions, the white stems should be tall and straight, leaves should be stiff and bright green. The flavor, though similar to a mild onion, is distinctly different. Texture is crisp when raw, tender after cooking.

Nutritional highlights: Low in calories and sodium; high in potassium; a good source of vitamins A and C and calcium.

Amount for 4 servings: 1 lb, about three or four tied in a bunch.

How to store: Well-wrapped in plastic in the refrigerator, leeks will keep for up to one week.

Basic prep: Remove green tops to within 2 inches of white section, and root tip. Peel outside layer of bulbs and small fibrous roots. Cut leeks in half lengthwise, then wash thoroughly under running water to remove grit and soil.

If using in salads, first parboil them for 8 to 10 minutes. Or serve thin slices in sandwiches of whole-wheat bread. They are especially good alongside potatoes: boil in salted water for about 12 to 15 minutes or until tender. Drain well. Leeks can also be left whole and baked, braised, microwaved or puréed.

Ways to serve: Simply buttered, with salt and pepper; or sprinkled with Parmesan cheese. Season with either basil, rosemary, thyme or ground ginger. Add diced leeks to quiche and egg dishes, casseroles, stews, stocks and soups — a famous one is Cock-a-Leekie Soup loved by the Scots.

Leek Fondue

Fondue is always a big hit at intimate dinner parties. The leeks in this recipe give the fondue a new and different spin. Serve with French bread cut into large cubes.

½ lb leeks (2 medium)
2 tablespoons butter or margarine
2 tablespoons unbleached all-purpose flour
1 cup flat beer
2½ cups grated Emmenthaler or Swiss cheese

1. Trim leeks, split lengthwise and rinse off all grit and soil. Chop finely.
2. In a saucepan, sauté leeks in butter for about 10 minutes, covered, until tender.
3. Stir in flour and cook 1 minute. Add beer, stirring constantly until mixture is thickened.
4. Gradually add cheese, stirring until cheese melts.
5. Pour into fondue pot or serving dish.

Makes 3 cups, about 6 servings.

Each serving contains about: 258 calories, 14g protein, 10g carbohydrate, 1g fiber, 17g fat, 53mg cholesterol, 171mg sodium.

Leek Toasts

Accompanied by a crisp salad, these toasts can be served as an elegant light luncheon dish for four people.

    1 lb (4 medium) leeks, cleaned, trimmed and chopped
    6 tablespoons butter or margarine (divided)
    1 tablespoon unbleached all-purpose flour
    ½ teaspoon white pepper
    ⅓ cup light cream or half-and-half
    1 egg yolk, lightly beaten
    1½ teaspoons fresh lemon juice
    4 slices white bread, crusts removed, cut in half diagonally

1. Cover leeks with water in a partially-lidded pan, and cook about 10 minutes or until tender. Drain and rinse under cold water.
2. Melt 3 tablespoons of the butter in another pan, add leeks, flour and pepper. Cook 1 minute.
3. Stir in cream and simmer, covered, about 10 minutes. Let cool slightly.
4. Stir egg yolk into leek mixture. Heat and stir for about 5 minutes, or until slightly thickened. Stir in lemon juice.
5. Melt remaining butter in pan and sauté bread on both sides, about 3 minutes.
6. Arrange toast halves on plates and spoon leeks on top. Garnish with a sprinkling of herbs, if desired.

Makes 4 servings.

Each serving contains about: 378 calories, 6g protein, 33g carbohydrate, 3g fiber, 26g fat, 122mg cholesterol, 349mg sodium.

Welsh Leek Pie

This is similar to a quiche Lorraine but without the need to make and roll out regular pie-crust. The biscuit baking mix forms its own crust during baking.

> 8 oz (2 large) leeks, cleaned and thinly sliced
> 1 (4-oz) can mushroom stems and pieces, drained
> ½ cup chopped onion
> 2 garlic cloves, finely minced
> 1 cup shredded Cheddar cheese
> 1½ cups milk
> ¾ cup reduced-fat biscuit baking mix
> 3 large eggs
> 1 teaspoon salt
> ¼ teaspoon freshly ground nutmeg
> ¼ teaspoon freshly ground black pepper

1. Coat a 10-inch pie plate with vegetable cooking spray. Preheat oven to 400 degrees F.
2. In a small pan, heat leeks and 1 inch water to boiling. Cook uncovered 5 minutes. Cover and cook until tender, 5 to 10 minutes. Drain well.
3. Mix leeks, mushrooms, onion, garlic and cheese in pie plate.
4. In a separate bowl whisk milk with baking mix, eggs and seasonings until smooth, about 1 minute. Pour into pie plate.
5. Bake at 400 degrees F for 30 to 35 minutes. Pie is done when knife inserted between center and edge comes out clean. Cool 5 minutes.

Makes one 10-inch pie, about 6 servings.

Each serving contains about: 238 calories, 12g protein, 21g carbohydrate, 3g fiber, 12g fat, 134mg cholesterol, 622mg sodium.

Lotus root

(Nelumbo lutea, N.nucifera or *Nymphaea lotus)*

Also known as: Renkon.

History and lore: Slicing the root crosswise reveals the beauty of the lotus as the small tunnels running its length create a decorative lacy pattern that makes an artistic addition to many dishes.

Lotus can be any of several different plants. The plant is an exotic one, the tuberous root of an Asian waterlily that grows in muddy ponds or paddies in the tropics. The lotus has been considered a delicacy in Oriental cuisine for over a thousand years, and is valued for its seeds, leaves and fragrant pink and white flowers as well as its root.

For centuries, lotus plants have been considered potent religious symbols, featured in legends and folk medicine. Since ancient times, the lotus represented fertility, birth, sexuality, purity and rebirth of the dead. Consequently the shape of the lotus was a popular motif in art, and is used symbolically in Hinduism and Buddhism. The lotus was a sacred flower to the people of Egypt, India and China, and is the national flower of India.

Ancient Greeks called several non-narcotic plants *lotos*, but when they referred to a lotus-eater they may have meant one who indulged in the opium poppy. Greek myths tell of a race of people called lotus-eaters who lived in North Africa and ate only the fruit and blossoms of the lotus tree. When others ate this magical food they forgot their homeland, family and friends. The crew of the hero Odysseus returning from the Trojan War, were lured to the Libyan coast to eat the fruit of the mysterious lotus. Overcome by dreamy forgetfulness, they had to be dragged back to the ship and chained to the rowing benches, for the homeward voyage. Even today, people who continually daydream are sometimes called lotus-eaters.

In Oriental medicine, lotus seeds are eaten to increase energy and vitality and to aid digestion. Small doses of lotus juice have been prescribed for tuberculosis, asthma, coughing, heart disease and enteritis.

Seasons when available: Fresh is available in fall and winter; canned or dried lotus, year-round.

What to look for when shopping: Check Asian food markets, health-food stores and some supermarkets for this delicacy. Select long firm roots with no bruises, blemishes or softness. Peel is brown, cream-colored or grayish-white; inside flesh should be ivory-colored. Texture is similar to a potato, but with a sweeter flavor. When fresh lotus is unavailable, look for ready-sliced lotus in cans, or dried in cello packages.

Nutritional highlights: Low in calories and sodium.

Amount for 4 servings: About 1 lb.

How to store: Keep whole roots in a cool dark place for up to one week; use any cut portion in 2 or 3 days.

Basic prep: Wash and peel fresh lotus, then slice ¼-inch thick. If inside surface of tunnels is dark, it is too old. To prevent discoloring after slicing, plunge into lightly salted water for 30 minutes before using. To reconstitute dried lotus, cover with boiling water, let stand for 30 minutes; drain.

Ways to serve: Lotus can be sautéed, stir-fried or deep-fried; or simmered till tender and vinegared as a simple pickle. Make pretty lotus chips for a party: slice thin rounds, dust with arrowroot powder or unbleached flour, deep-fry until crisp, then sprinkle with sea-salt.

Lotus Root Tempura

A good tempura can be made with many vegetables, such as zucchini, sweet potatoes and carrots, all cut in thin slices. Lotus root, with its lacy design, looks especially pretty because holes appear in the batter after frying. If fresh lotus is unavailable, substitute a 19-oz can, found in most Oriental markets; drain and rinse before use.

Tempura batter (see recipe below)
1 lb fresh lotus root
Oil for frying (about 1 cup)

1. Make batter.
2. While batter is resting, cut lotus into ½-inch slices.
3. Heat oil in pan sufficient for deep-frying.
4. Dip slices of lotus root in batter and fry until light brown.
5. Drain well on paper towel and serve immediately.

Tempura batter (makes 3 cups)

    2 cups unbleached all-purpose flour
    1 cup stale flat beer (must be flat, or batter becomes too foamy)
    1 cup water
    3 egg yolks
    ¼ teaspoon salt

Blend all ingredients. Let mixture sit for about ½ hour.

Makes 4 servings.

Each serving contains about: 504 calories, 12g protein, 70g carbohydrate, 3g fiber, 21g fat, 159mg cholesterol, 190mg sodium.

Sweet and Sour Lotus Root

Crunchy-coated lotus root in a sweet and sour sauce is a delightfully exotic side dish. Szechuan peppercorns can be found in all Oriental markets; if unobtainable, don't substitute anything else, as flavors would not be identical.

    1 teaspoon Szechuan peppercorns (optional)
    3 tablespoons sesame oil
    12 oz fresh lotus root, peeled (or canned)
    3 tablespoons rice vinegar
    2 tablespoons granulated sugar
    2 tablespoons soy sauce
    ½ cup mock-chicken flavored stock (½ teaspoon bouillon powder in
        ½ cup water)
    1½ teaspoons cornstarch dissolved in 1½ tablespoons water

1. Sauté peppercorns in sesame oil for 1 minute or until they darken. Remove peppercorns with a slotted spoon.
2. Add lotus root to oil and mix in rice vinegar, sugar, soy sauce and stock. Toss and cook for 1 minute.
3. Stir in dissolved cornstarch, and cook until sauce becomes thick.

Makes 4 servings.

Each serving contains about: 174 calories, 3g protein, 23g carbohydrate, 1g fiber, 10g fat, 0mg cholesterol, 689mg sodium.

Stuffed Lotus Root Sandwiches

Make these immediately before you are ready to serve dinner, with your rice cooked and kept warm, and your tea steeping; then the oil won't soak into the lotus root.

   2 lbs fresh lotus root, peeled (or use canned)
   1 medium onion, chopped
   ½ lb fresh mushrooms, washed and chopped
   1 teaspoon grated fresh ginger root
   1 garlic clove, minced
   White of 1 large egg, well beaten
   2 tablespoons soy sauce
   1½ tablespoons vegetable oil
   Batter (see recipe below)
   Oil for frying (about 1 cup)

1. Cut lotus root into ⅛-inch slices. Set aside.
2. Prepare filling: mix together mushrooms, onion, ginger, garlic, egg white, soy sauce and the 1½ tablespoons vegetable oil.
3. Spread filling evenly over one slice of lotus root and cover with another slice, sandwich style.
4. Prepare batter.
5. Dip "sandwiches" into batter, let set and dip again.
6. Fry in hot oil until golden brown, then drain well on paper towels and serve hot.

Batter (makes about 1 cup)

   1 large egg, well beaten
   ½ cup water
   ½ cup unbleached all-purpose flour

Beat egg with water. Blend in flour until smooth.

Makes 8 servings.

Each serving contains about: 216 calories, 6g protein, 29g carbohydrate, 2g fiber, 12g fat, 26mg cholesterol, 320mg sodium.

M

Malanga

(*Xanthosoma* species)   See also Taro.

Also known as: Malanga blanca; Malanga amarilla; Malanga lila; Yautia; Yautia amarilla; Yautia blanca; Tannia; Tannier; Coco-yam. (Note: *malanga isleña* sold in Cuban markets is actually taro.)

History and lore: This root has several names and a variety of species all native to the American tropics. (Because the tuber closely resembles taro, there is much confusion between the two.) Spanish-speaking Cubans, for instance, call the vegetable malanga; Puerto Ricans know it as yautia; people in Central and South America call it tannia and tannier; East Africans refer to it as maduma; West Africans know it as coco-yam.

Malanga is the edible cormel (similar to a tuber) of a plant called *Xanthosoma sagittifolium*, common in tropical areas such as Caribbean, Central and South America, Africa and Southeast Asia. When travels take you to these corners of the world, be sure to visit the bustling local produce markets to see the cheap and plentiful displays of unusual root vegetables. Malanga is as popular in the tropics as the potato is in North America.

In the United States where immigrants from Puerto Rico, Cuba and Trinidad have settled, their foods can be found in area supermarkets, so produce sections stock malanga, boniato, cassava, taro and tropical yam, imported from the Caribbean.

Seasons when available: Year-round.

What to look for when shopping: Check in Hispanic, Puerto Rican, or West Indian markets, or large supermarkets. Malanga has thin shaggy patchy brown skin, and is shaped somewhat like a sweet potato, long and curved or club-shaped, about 6 inches long. Varieties are separated by flesh color: Malanga blanca is white-fleshed, malanga lila is pink inside and malanga amarilla is yellow-fleshed. All varieties have a nutty earthy flavor and a waxy, starchy consistency after cooking. Look for paler tubers that are very firm, without wrinkled, soft or moldy patches.

Nutritional highlights: High in calories, at 270 per cup after cooking. A good source of vitamin C and iron.

Amount for 4 servings: 1 lb, about 2 medium size.

How to store: Tropical roots don't take well to refrigeration, and are best eaten fresh. Store malanga at room temperature and use within five days.

Basic prep: Do not serve raw. Malanga must be cooked before eating. Wash and scrub well under cold running water. Trim off top and tail, and pare away skin and any soft patches. Rinse and cover with cold water to prevent discoloration.

Boil chunks in salted water until tender, about 20 minutes. Or bake in the oven, or drizzle with olive oil and grill on the outdoor barbecue.

Ways to serve: Serve as you would potatoes, simply with butter, salt and freshly ground pepper, or diced in potato-style salads, or puréed for an interesting side vegetable seasoned with a dash of nutmeg. Add a few small pieces to soups and stews, or slice and fry them to make chips or fritters.

Pan-Roasted Malanga

Roasting intensifies the flavors of vegetables, since some of their moisture evaporates in the oven. It helps to conserve vitamins, which often get poured down the drain when vegetables are boiled in water. Oven-baking also makes roots taste sweeter because intense heat caramelizes some of their natural sugars. Leftovers are great cold as is, or added to salads, or reheated in the microwave.

  1 lb malanga (about 2 medium size)
  ½ lb parsnips
  ½ lb turnips
  ½ lb rutabagas
  1 lb sweet onions (2 large)
  ½ cup olive oil
  Juice of 1 lemon
  1 teaspoon crushed dried rosemary
  ½ teaspoon salt
  ½ teaspoon freshly ground black pepper

1. Scrub and peel vegetables. Cut malanga, parsnips, turnips and rutabagas into 1-inch chunks, and onions into wedges.
2. Spread vegetables in a single layer in 1 or 2 baking pans.
3. Drizzle with olive oil and lemon juice. Sprinkle with rosemary, salt and pepper.
4. Bake at 450 degrees F, turning every 10 minutes, for 30 minutes or until lightly browned and tender.

Makes 6 servings.

Each serving contains about: 376 calories, 4g protein, 51g carbohydrate, 6g fiber, 18g fat, 0mg cholesterol, 216mg sodium.

O

Onion

(*Allium* genus)   See also its cousins: Garlic, Leek, Scallion, Shallot.

History and lore: The Allium family is a large one: well over 300 species of onion, 70 of which are natives of North America, varying in strength of taste and smell. This odorous group includes scallions, shallots, leeks, onions and garlic, all familiar roots in the kitchen.

Are onions in fact roots? Purists would argue the onion is both stem and leaf: the concentric shells of onion tissue are the swollen bases of last year's leaves, storing nutrients for the following year's growth. But where would cooks be without these fragrant bulbs?

The onion's origins go back so far in time that no one knows its wild ancestors. When primitive humans were still hunter-gatherers, they could sniff out the wild bulb, making it easy to collect. It was native to a broad region stretching from Israel to India, and has been cultivated in the Middle East and Southwest Asia since at least 3000 B.C. The onion has since starred in almost every cuisine on earth.

The word onion probably derived from the Latin "unus" meaning "one." Ancient Egyptians regarded the root with its concentric circles as a symbol of the universe and an object of worship: an Egyptian mummy was found still clutching the sacred bulb. Romans "knew their onions," and spread onion-growing across Europe to Britain after their armies had marched across the land. By Elizabethan times, the favorite vegetables of England were onions and leeks, and popular salads were composed of onions and herbs.

Long before the arrival of European adventurers and settlers in the Americas, native peoples were adding highly pungent wild onions to their diet: a region around the southern shore of Lake Michigan was so thick with sulfur-smelling wild onions the local Menominee tribe named it *shika'ko* ("skunk place"), the origin of the city of Chicago. When American cowboys were later riding the range and making their "son-of-a-bitch stew," an indispensable ingredient was the native onion they called a "skunk egg."

In the old days, folk medicine in central Europe prescribed onions for insomnia, colds, laryngitis, earache, warts and animal bites. Modern researchers are still suggesting the fragrant bulb has medicinal properties: eating a raw white onion every day may help increase patients' beneficial HDL cholesterol, so onions can rightfully play an important part in a wholesome low-calorie, low-fat heart-healthy diet.

Seasons when available: Year-round. Warmer climates and summer-maturing types produce varieties with milder sweeter flavor.

What to look for when shopping: Firm, well-shaped bulbs, with dry papery skins and no soft spots, seed stems, sprouts or areas of black powder.

Globe (Yellow or Golden) can be white, yellow or red, with a strong flavor for stews; Bermuda are large, flattish, with white or yellow flesh and mild flavor; Red or Italian onions are flattish, with red skins and mild flavor.

In summer, look for fresh varieties such as Vidalias from Georgia, Maui from Hawaii, Walla Walla from Washington, and the 1015 from Texas, all mild-flavored to eat raw.

Boiling/pearl/cocktail/pickling onions are not distinct varieties, but small round white onions harvested when about one-inch or less in diameter.

Nutritional highlights: Low in calories, fat and sodium, and high in potassium.

Amount for 4 servings: About 1½ lbs. Mesh-bags holding 3 lbs are often the best buy. Boiling/pearl onions are frequently sold in small baskets.

How to store: Bulk supplies store up to one month in a mesh-type bag hung somewhere airy, dry and cool. The sweet summer varieties have a shorter life, no more than two weeks. Never store onions with potatoes: they will rapidly decay. For day to day needs, keep a supply in the refrigerator (where chilling completely subdues fumes that make you cry). Keep them away from milk or butter, to avoid transfering flavor. Seal cut onions tightly in cello-wrap, refrigerate, and use within 3 days.

Basic prep: No need to weep over onions: be sure they are *well chilled*. Give them 2 hours in the refrigerator or 10 minutes in the freezer before skinning, chopping or slicing.

Use mild varieties raw in salads and sandwiches. Onions take to all styles of cooking: baking, boiling, braising, frying, glazing, sautéing, stir-frying.

And all shapes: minced, cut in dice, chunks, wedges, halves or left whole. They pair up beautifully with so many other root vegetables, in soups, stews, pilafs and scalloped dishes.

Use boiling/pearl onions in stews, in pickles and for serving in a cream sauce. Boil onions until tender: 15 minutes for small; 30 minutes for large; drain well. Extra-large onions are fabulous left whole and baked in a microwave or conventional oven, stuffed or not. The longer you cook onions, the milder they become. Long baking or oven-roasting, brings out delicious sweetness and caramelizes the natural sugars.

Ways to serve: Make the legendary French onion soup, fit for a King of France. Or add chopped onions and garlic to a hearty breaddough or a cornbread-muffin batter for brunch or lunch. Microwave onion halves for 2 minutes, with 2 tablespoons water, a sprinkling of dried sage, black pepper and Parmesan cheese; top with dabs of butter before serving.

Fruit and Veggie Pilaf

This terrific mixture of fruits and vegetables, combined with brown rice, can be a main course or side dish.

    2 tablespoons butter or margarine
    1 large onion
    1 cup grated carrots
    1 cup long-grain brown rice
    2½ cups vegetable stock (see page 20)
    ¼ cup *each* raisins, chopped dried apricots, chopped pitted dates and
        cashews

1. Melt butter in a 2-quart saucepan. Add onion and carrot, and cook until soft, about 5 minutes.
2. Add rice to pan and when it begins to brown add stock, fruit and nuts.
3. Cover and simmer for about 45 minutes, or until rice is tender.

Makes 6 servings.

Each serving contains about: 263 calories, 5g protein, 45g carbohydrate, 4g fiber, 8g fat, 12mg cholesterol, 73mg sodium.

Spinach-Stuffed Onions

As the onions cook, the seam disappears and the onions appear to be whole, stuffed with the savory filling.

> 4 large white onions (about 2 lbs)
> ¼ cup chopped fresh mushrooms
> 1 (10-oz) box frozen chopped spinach, thawed and drained
> 2 large eggs, lightly beaten
> ½ lb ricotta cheese
> ¾ cup grated Parmesan cheese (divided)
> ¼ teaspoon dried marjoram
> ⅛ teaspoon grated nutmeg
> 2 cups tomato sauce

1. Split onions in half lengthwise and peel. Place in boiling water for about 20 minutes. Drain.
2. Pull onions apart, layer by layer. Chop onion pieces that are too small to be stuffed, and place in a bowl.
3. Make stuffing: to the chopped onions add mushrooms, spinach, eggs, ricotta, ¼ cup of the Parmesan, marjoram and nutmeg. Mix well.
4. Pour 1 cup of the tomato sauce to cover bottom of a large flat casserole dish.
5. On each onion skin put a heaping tablespoon of stuffing mixture, and roll up. Place them in the casserole seam-side down (touching but not packed too tightly). Pour over remaining tomato sauce.
6. Cover and bake at 350 degrees F for 30 minutes.
7. Remove cover and sprinkle with remaining Parmesan. Bake uncovered 15 minutes more, until sauce is bubbly.

Makes 4 servings.

Each serving contains about: 320 calories, 23g protein, 30g carbohydrate, 6g fiber, 13g fat, 138mg cholesterol, 545mg sodium.

Baked White Onions with Mango Chutney

Onions need not be relegated to seasoning other food. Here is a piquant side dish that's simple to prepare. Mango chutney is found in most supermarkets.

3 large sweet white Bermuda onions, peeled
1 tablespoon honey
1 tablespoon teriyaki sauce
½ cup mock-chicken stock (½ teaspoon granules in ½ cup water)
1 jar (about 8-oz) mango chutney

1. Cut each onion in half crosswise. Place cut-side down in a shallow greased pan (or a pan coated with nonstick cooking spray).
2. Mix honey, teriyaki sauce and chicken stock, and spoon over onions.
3. Bake at 350 degrees F for about 20 minutes, until tops are golden.
4. Spoon chutney on each plate and arrange onion-half on top.

Makes 6 servings.

Each serving contains about: 112 calories, 1g protein, 28g carbohydrate, 2g fiber, 1g fat, 0mg cholesterol, 223mg sodium.

Drunken Onions

A great dish to prepare when perhaps you have a leftover cup of wine or vermouth, and want to add a stylish accent to dinner.

2 tablespoons olive oil
6 white onions (of equal medium size), peeled
1 cup red wine or vermouth

1. Put oil and onions in a flameproof ovenproof pan over low heat. When oil begins to sizzle, add wine and boil a few seconds.
2. Add water to come half-way up onions. Transfer pan to oven.
3. Bake at 325 degrees F for about 1 hour.
4. Return to stovetop and heat until sauce is thick and syrupy. Remove from heat and serve.

Makes 6 servings.

Each serving contains about: 129 calories, 2g protein, 14g carbohydrate, 3g fiber, 5g fat, 0mg cholesterol, 7mg sodium.

Sage-Buttered Pearl Onions

The beauty of this dish is its speed and simplicity, but fresh sage is imperative. It is usually sold in bags in most supermarket vegetable aisles, unless you are fortunate enough to grow your own.

16 pearl/boiling onions, peeled
⅓ cup butter or margarine
1 cup chopped fresh sage, leaves only

1. In a microwave casserole dish, place the onions about 1 inch apart. Dot each one with about ½ teaspoon butter. Sprinkle chopped sage over onions.
2. Cover and microwave on HIGH for about 10 to 12 minutes or until tender when pierced.

Makes 4 servings.

Each serving contains about: 171 calories, 1g protein, 8g carbohydrate, 2g fiber, 15g fat, 41mg cholesterol, 164mg sodium.

Pearl Onion Kabobs

Kabobs on the barbecue are fun to make any time of year. For exceptional flavor, marinate the vegetables in a special dressing before grilling.

Sweet-sour dressing (see recipe below)
16 pearl/boiling onions, peeled
16 cherry-size tomatoes
16 medium-size mushrooms, cleaned, stems removed
1 small eggplant, cubed into 16 pieces about 1½ inches
4 long metal skewers

1. Prepare dressing.
2. Place all vegetables in a glass bowl and pour sufficient dressing to coat and marinate them while coals are getting hot.
3. Place vegetables on skewers, alternating each one.
4. Place over coals and cook until vegetables are soft. Baste with additional dressing if desired.
5. Serve with steamed rice.

Sweet-sour dressing (makes about 2½ cups)

    1 cup canola oil
    ½ cup honey
    ½ cup vinegar
    ⅓ cup ketchup
    1 teaspoon Worcestershire sauce
    1 garlic clove, minced

Place all ingredients in food processor. Purée until smooth.

Makes 4 servings.

Each serving contains about: 722 calories, 4g protein, 61g carbohydrate, 6g fiber, 55g fat, 0mg cholesterol, 276mg sodium.

Onion Biscuits

These zesty-flavored biscuits can be topped with cheeses, a cream cheese spread or smoked salmon. They freeze very well: cool to room temperature on a wire-rack then place individual biscuits on cookie sheets and freeze. When frozen, bag them together in airtight plastic wrap and return to freezer.

    2 large eggs, well beaten
    2 large yellow onions, grated
    ½ cup canola oil
    3 cups unbleached all-purpose flour
    2 teaspoons baking powder
    1 teaspoon sugar
    ½ cup poppy seeds or sesame seeds
    2 tablespoons water

1. In a bowl whisk eggs; add onions and oil.
2. Sift in dry ingredients. Add poppy seeds and water. Mix well.
3. Drop the mixture by tablespoonsful onto lightly greased cookie sheets.
4. Bake at 400 degrees F for 10 to 15 minutes until nicely brown.

Makes 40 appetizer-size biscuits.

Each biscuit contains about: 75 calories, 2g protein, 8g carbohydrate, 1g fiber, 4g fat, 11mg cholesterol, 20mg sodium.

Cornish Onion and Apple Pie

This recipe comes from the county of Cornwall, in the southwest corner of England. Onions and apples may seem an unusual combination, but try it and you'll find they work well together!

    Pastry for a double-crust 9-inch pie (see recipe below)
    4 green apples, peeled, cored and thinly sliced
    4 medium-size yellow onions, peeled and chopped
    3 tablespoons butter or margarine
    2 teaspoons fresh sage, finely chopped
    ¼ teaspoon ground allspice

1. Make pastry and divide dough in half. Roll out and line pan.
2. Cover bottom with a layer of apples. Add a layer of onion, a few dabs of butter, some sage and a dash of allspice. Keep layering until ingredients are finished, ending with a little butter on top.
3. Roll out second half of dough and place over filling. Seal and flute edges decoratively. Put two small gashes in center of pie for steam to escape.
4. Bake at 375 degrees F for 50 to 60 minutes.

Pastry (for one 9-inch double-crust pie)

    ⅔ cup butter or margarine
    1½ teaspoons granulated sugar
    ¼ teaspoon salt
    2 cups unbleached all-purpose or pastry flour
    3 tablespoons ice water

1. Mix all ingredients. Chill in freezer for about ½ hour.
2. Divide dough into two. Roll one half and place in 9-inch pie pan.

Makes one 9-inch pie, about 8 servings.

Each serving contains about: 358 calories, 4g protein, 41g carbohydrate, 3g fiber, 20g fat, 53mg cholesterol, 270mg sodium.

P

Parsley root

(Petroselinum crispum, var. *tuberosum)*

Also known as: Turnip-rooted parsley; Rooted parsley; Hamburg parsley; Dutch parsley; Heimischer.

History and lore: We tend to think of parsley as endowed only with flavorful leaves: plain, curly, the rarely grown fern-leaf and celery-leaf parsley, but a fifth variety is valued for its turnip-like root. Parsley root is sometimes known as Hamburg parsley, and the Germans called it Dutch parsley, so it was probably developed by Dutch farmers.

Parsley has been around Europe for centuries: native to the Mediterranean, it was first grown in Sardinia and Southern Italy. The leaves were enjoyed by the ancient Romans and Greeks who fashioned them into garlands to crown military heroes and honor top athletes. And to this day, the root is a popular vegetable added to the hearty soups of Northern Europe, including Germany, Holland and Poland. Now that farmers are growing it in California, New Jersey and Texas, it is turning up more frequently on restaurant menus.

Seasons when available: Fall, winter and spring (August through April), with peak supply in January.

What to look for when shopping: The roots, white or creamy-beige, should be firm and smooth; small to medium size are best. They are sometimes sold with their feathery green leaves, which should look fresh (not wilted or yellowed). Although the roots appear similar to parsnips, the tops clearly have the parsley aroma. The root flavor is mildly earthy, similar to celeriac, with a crisp texture.

125

Nutritional highlights: High in fiber and vitamin C.

Amount for 4 servings: About ¾ lb.

How to store: Leave tops untrimmed. Wrap well in cellophane and store in the refrigerator; they should keep for a week or 10 days.

Basic prep: Scrub the root well. Peel or not, as you please. Remove leafy tops and add to soups as a flavoring. Leave small roots whole; slice or dice the larger ones. Boil in salted water until tender, or add to braises and hearty stews with carrots, leeks, mushrooms and potatoes.

Ways to serve: Simply as a side vegetable, with seasoned butter. Or make a delicious purée, spiked with herbs or blended with mashed potatoes.

Parsley Root Chips

The beauty of parsley root is that you can use the whole thing, leaves and all, and here it makes tempting nibbles for an appetizer tray.

   3 parsley roots, peeled and thinly sliced
   Juice of 1 lemon
   Oil for frying (about ½ cup)
   Salt and pepper to taste

1. Remove sprigs from parsley roots, wash and pat dry. Reserve sprigs for garnish.
2. Heat oil in frying pan. When hot, drop in root slices and fry until golden brown, about 30 seconds. Drain chips on paper towels.
3. Drop parsley leaves into hot oil for a few seconds and remove before they turn brown. Drain well.
4. Season chips and leaf garnish with salt and pepper. Serve hot.

Makes 4 appetizer servings.

Each serving contains about: 112 calories, 3g protein, 7g carbohydrate, 4g fiber, 8g fat, 0mg cholesterol, 144mg sodium.

Dutch Parsley Soup

Parsley root adds an interesting herbal flavor to this velvety soup. Serve warm not hot, to avoid curdling the cream, along with a crisp salad and crusty French bread. Granules for mock-chicken stock are sold in health-food stores.

¼ cup (½ stick) butter or margarine
½ cup onion, chopped
3 medium parsley roots, peeled and cubed
7 cups mock-chicken stock (1 teaspoon granules for each cup water)
2 medium potatoes, peeled and cubed
1 medium parsnip, peeled and cubed
1 cup whipping cream
Salt and freshly ground black pepper to taste

1. In a soup pot, melt butter and sauté onion for 3 to 4 minutes until translucent.
2. Pour in stock and remaining vegetables.
3. Bring to boil, then reduce heat, cover and simmer for about 50 minutes, until vegetables are tender.
4. Transfer to food processor in batches and purée.
5. Return to soup pot, and add cream, salt and pepper. Rewarm a few minutes over gentle heat.

Makes 8 servings.

Each serving contains about: 213 calories, 4g protein, 15g carbohydrate, 3g fiber, 16g fat, 49mg cholesterol, 1059mg sodium.

Stuffed Peppers with Parsley Root

Parsley root adds a special taste to these stuffed peppers. Serve them as is, or with a cream sauce or fresh tomato sauce.

2 cups parsley root, peeled and diced
½ cup onion, finely chopped
1 garlic clove, finely minced
¼ cup (½ stick) butter or margarine
2 cups fine dry bread crumbs
2 large eggs, well beaten
¾ teaspoon crushed dried thyme
½ teaspoon freshly ground black pepper
6 large green bell peppers, tops removed and seeded

1. Sauté parsley root, onion and garlic in butter, until onion is translucent and parsley root is soft.
2. In a separate bowl, mix bread crumbs, eggs, thyme and black pepper, and add parsley root mixture. Mix well.
3. Spoon mixture into peppers and stand them in a baking dish. Cover dish with foil.
4. Bake at 350 degrees F for 30 minutes. Remove foil and bake another 10 minutes.

Makes 6 servings.

Each serving contains about: 262 calories, 8g protein, 33g carbohydrate, 4g fiber, 11g fat, 93mg cholesterol, 351mg sodium.

Parsnip

(Pastinaca sativa)

History and lore: Ogden Nash once rhymed:
Some people call the parsnip edible.
Myself, I find this claim incredible.

Parsnips are native to the Rhine Valley and north-eastern Europe, known and used as food since the Early Christian era; the Roman Emperor Tiberius was said to enjoy cakes made with parsnips, fruit and honey. Parsnips were more popular than carrots during the Middle Ages, especially when fast days such as Lent were rigorously observed. Hieronymus Trager, the German botanist wrote in 1551 that parsnips and fava beans were the basic Lenten food; parsnip flour was used for bread; and sweet parsnips were given to infants being weaned. The popularity of parsnips in Europe didn't begin to wane until the potato arrived from America.

The first parsnips in the Americas were brought to Venezuela and Peru in the late 16th century and to Virginia in the early 17th century, where early settlers put the first crops into parsnip cakes and puddings. Parsnips are now found growing wild throughout North America, Europe and temperate areas of Asia.

The most sugary varieties of parsnips were once boiled down into syrup, and left in tubs with yeast and "loaf sugar" to ferment into wine. Since this primarily winter-vegetable becomes sweeter the later it is harvested, old-time cookbook writers would instruct makers of parsnip-wine to harvest their roots in the spring for the best fermentation.

Seasons when available: Fresh ones are in peak supply (and at their sweetest) during winter, after the cold has converted their starch to sugars. Cello-packed bags are available year-round.

What to look for when shopping: Long tapering creamy-white roots. Choose firm, smooth and uncracked roots, without rootlets or discolored patches. Flavor should be sweet and nutty. Older roots may have tough woody cores.

Nutritional highlights: More vitamin C than its carrot cousin, and high in potassium, the root is low in calories and sodium.

Amount for 4 servings: About 2 lb.

How to store: Trim off the tops, and refrigerate roots unwashed in a plastic bag, for a week or 10 days. Keep them from apples, pears and other fruits, including tomatoes, as ethylene from these fruits causes roots to become bitter.

For longer storage, wash, peel and cube parsnips, blanch in boiling water for 2 minutes then freeze; or fully cook whole parsnips then freeze. Frozen parsnips in plastic bags keep up to 8 months.

Basic prep: Scrub with a vegetable brush under running water to remove dirt. Peel and cut lengthwise or into segments (tops are wider and take longer to cook than tips).

Ways to serve: Cook in 1-inch boiling water about 20 minutes or until tender. Or steam parsnips like carrots; mash them like turnips. Or add to stocks, soups, stews and purées to give a subtle sweetness. For delicious purées, cook half parsnips half carrots, and blend together with a little butter and a pinch of freshly grated nutmeg. Oven-roast parsnip chunks, or grill them on the outdoor barbecue.

Parsnip Mock-Crab Salad

Would you believe raw parsnips can taste like crab or lobster? Try them in this salad, and we think you'll agree.

    2 large parsnips, peeled and grated
    3 tablespoons fresh lemon juice
    1 cup commercial low-calorie mayonnaise
    1 teaspoon Dijon-style mustard
    1 teaspoon Worcestershire sauce
    3 cups salad greens
    1 cup thinly sliced celery
    ½ cup chopped walnuts
    3 large eggs, hardboiled, sliced
    3 scallions, trimmed and sliced

1. Toss parsnips in lemon juice in a small bowl. Set aside.
2. In another small bowl mix mayonnaise with mustard and Worcestershire sauce. Set aside.
3. Line six plates with salad greens. On each plate arrange equal portions of parsnips, celery, walnuts, eggs and scallions.
4. Top each salad with a scoop of mayonnaise mixture. Serve cold.

Makes 6 servings.

Each serving contains about: 204 calories, 6g protein, 15g carbohydrate, 3g fiber, 14g fat, 126mg cholesterol, 126mg sodium.

Julie's Algerian-Style Parsnips with Couscous

Sandra is justifiably proud of the culinary skills of her daughter Julie; this is one of her favorite recipes. Couscous can be found in most health-food and specialty stores, and the gourmet section of some supermarkets. Follow couscous package directions as some types cook in less than 20 minutes.

1 cup regular or whole-wheat couscous
5½ cups water (divided)
1 (16-oz) can tomato sauce
½ medium onion, minced
1 garlic clove, minced
1 medium parsnip, peeled and sliced
1 small turnip, peeled and cubed
2 ribs celery, thickly sliced
2 medium carrots, thickly sliced
1 medium yellow summer squash, sliced
1 medium zucchini, sliced
1 (15-oz) can garbanzo beans (chick peas)

1. In a pan bring 2 cups of the water to boil, and add couscous. Reduce heat and let cook for about 20 minutes (or follow package directions), until all water has been absorbed. Set aside, and keep warm.
2. In a large pan mix the remaining 3½ cups water with tomato sauce. Add vegetables and garbanzo beans, and cook about 20 to 30 minutes, until vegetables are tender.
3. Place warm couscous on a large serving platter and spoon vegetables over the top.

Makes 4 servings.

Each serving contains about: 358 calories, 13g protein, 74g carbohydrate, 17g fiber, 2g fat, 0mg cholesterol, 427mg sodium.

Parsnip Fritters

Serve these fritters as a main dish with Onion-Mushroom Sauce (page 141) or simply a white sauce. Delicious!

  5 large parsnips, scraped and quartered
  3 tablespoons unbleached all-purpose flour
  ¼ cup minced onion
  4 tablespoons melted butter or margarine
  1 teaspoon garlic powder
  2 large eggs, beaten
  Oil for frying (about 1 cup)

1. Cook parsnips in boiling water for about 15 to 20 minutes, or until tender. Drain well.
2. Put parsnips, flour, onion, butter and garlic powder in food processor and purée. Stir in beaten eggs.
3. Form into cakes. If too moist, add a little more flour.
4. Fry in oil until brown on both sides. Drain well on paper towel.

Makes 4 servings.

Each serving (without sauce) contains about: 436 calories, 6g protein, 36g carbohydrate, 8g fiber, 31g fat, 137mg cholesterol, 166mg sodium.

Pineapple Baked Parsnips

Pineapple goes surprisingly well with sweet young parsnips, and gives them an Hawaiian flair. Serve them at your next luau.

1½ teaspoons cornstarch
2 tablespoons brown sugar
½ cup pineapple juice
1½ lbs parsnips, peeled and cut into julienne strips
2 tablespoons butter or margarine
1 (8-oz) can pineapple chunks

1. In a mixing bowl, combine cornstarch, brown sugar and pineapple juice. Stir until smooth.
2. Place parsnips in an ungreased 11½ x 7½ x 1½-inch baking pan and pour pineapple-juice mixture over parsnips. Dot with butter and arrange pineapple chunks over the top.
3. Bake at 350 degrees F for 45 minutes to 1 hour, until bubbly and parsnips are tender.

Makes 4 servings.

Each serving contains about: 258 calories, 2g protein, 51g carbohydrate, 8g fiber, 6g fat, 15mg cholesterol, 79mg sodium.

Potato

(Solanum tuberosum)

Also known as: Irish potato; *Pratie* (Irish); *Papa* (Quechuan); *Patata* (Spanish).

History and lore: No, it's not a root, but it goes with so many other roots and makes an significant contribution in the kitchen.

Our friend the potato is produced in 130 of the world's 167 independent countries; hardy and adaptable, it grows from below sea level behind Dutch dikes to almost 14,000 feet in the Andes and Himalayas. Andean farmers cultivate as many as 3,000 of the 5,000 or so potato varieties, embracing all eight species.

Before 6,000 B.C. nomadic Indians on the central Andean plateau collected wild potatoes, and peoples of Peru have been cultivating their native tuber since 3,000 B.C., using it in the form of *chuño*, a product made by alternate freezing, pounding and dehydrating. They milled chuño into a fine flour and used it to make a sort of bread. The potato was such a vital food staple in the high Andes that the Incas worshipped it as a spirit god and placed chuño in the tombs of the dead as food for their journey to the Afterworld.

Brought to Europe in the 16th century, the potato had a mixed reception at first. Rumors said it caused leprosy, perhaps because it looked bumpy and sometimes scabrous. Others, knowing it belonged to the poisonous nightshade family, declared it dangerous to eat; confused cooks were mistakenly cooking the leaves and discarding the tubers. (Potatoes grown in the Renaissance would not have killed anyone, but they did sometimes cause people to have a skin rash, not leprosy, probably because of the higher solanine content at that time.) Russian peasants, as late as the 18th century, died of famine rather than cultivate spuds. Then there were religious groups believing potatoes were powerful sex stimulants; Presbyterian ministers in Scotland considered them unholy and not to be eaten because they were not mentioned in the Bible.

But within eighty years or so of its discovery in Peru, the potato became firmly established in Ireland, probably because it was easy to grow, and simple to cook in a single kettle over a peat fire. While Europeans gradually accepted the potato, the Irish poor became completely dependent on it, so when potato blight struck in 1845, it resulted in widespread famine, disease and death — and mass migration to the U.S.

With the plant disease contained, healthy crops could be produced around the world (although a return of the blight still poses a threat); but people today are no longer dependent on it as their sole food source.

Seasons when available: Year-round. Quality tends to be better in winter months.

What to look for when shopping: All varieties should be firm; brown skin (Russet, best for baking, frying), creamy white or red skin (White Rose and Round Red, best for boiling, mashing, frying, roasting). Avoid any with soft spots, and wilted, wrinkled or green skins; they will spoil and discolor quickly, and taste bitter. Newer varieties with fresh taste, hybridized from different sources in South America, are yellow, gold, purple and pink skinned (such as Yellow Finnish, Yukon Gold, Delta Gold, Peruvian Blue, Purple or All Blue). Yellows have a moist buttery flavor; purples are similar to Russets in flavor.

"New" potatoes are freshly dug, and not a separate variety.

Nutritional highlights: Low in calories and sodium, high in complex carbohydrates.

Amount for 4 servings: 4 medium or 10 small, about 1½ lbs.

How to store: Don't buy more than you can use in two weeks. Keep potatoes unwashed in a paper sack or airy basket in a cool dark well-ventilated place, not the refrigerator.

Basic prep: Scrub potatoes with a vegetable brush under cold running water. Remove any soft, discolored or green areas, any "eyes" and sprouting. Green indicates solanine may be present; although cooking reduces the danger of solanine (large amounts can make you sick), it's best to remove any you see.

For boiling and mashing: cut potatoes into large chunks, cover with cold water, and bring to boil; cooking time varies with density of potato and the size of pieces, 20 to 30 minutes.

For regular-oven baking: Prick with fork to allow steam to escape; insert a "baking nail" in center, to hasten cooking. For soft skins, wrap each potato in aluminum foil. Allow 1 to 1¼ hours at 350 degrees F depending on size.

For microwaving: 1 potato, well pricked and wrapped in wax-paper, takes 8 minutes. Rotate after 4 minutes.

Ways to serve: The list is endless; other books devoted entirely to spuds present hundreds of ways: in chowders smooth or chunky, in soups, stews, salads, breads and pies. Potatoes are good with most fresh or dried herbs. Give potatoes a new spin with purée blends of cooked potatoes and parsnips, carrots or fennel.

Goat Cheese and Potato Tarts

Irresistible appetizers, with the robust flavor of the cheese softened and mellowed by the mild-tasting potatoes.

Pastry (see recipe below)
2 large (about 12 oz) Russet potatoes, peeled and quartered
½ cup whipping cream
10 oz goat cheese cut into 10 slices
¼ cup minced chives

1. Make pastry, roll dough into 8 rounds and press into tart pans (2½-inch muffin pans).
2. Bake tart shells at 350 degrees F until golden, approximately 15 min.
3. Boil potatoes in water for about 12 to 15 minutes, or until tender. Drain.
4. Blend potatoes with cream and two cheese slices until smooth.
5. Fill tart shells with potato mixture and top each with a piece of cheese.
6. Bake at 350 degrees F for 20 minutes, until cheese is melted.
7. Garnish with a sprinkle of minced chives.

Pastry

1¾ cups unbleached all-purpose flour
½ cup butter or margarine
1 egg yolk
4 tablespoons cold water

1. Mix flour and butter until mixture is like coarse crumbs. Add egg yolk and water, and form dough.
2. Wrap and refrigerate for about 45 minutes.

Makes 8 2½-inch appetizer tarts.

Each tart contains about: 370 calories, 9g protein, 29g carbohydrate, 1g fiber, 25g fat, 112mg cholesterol, 297mg sodium.

Potato Samosas

This appetizer or finger food has an East Indian flavor. Samosas are generally fried, but baking them reduces the fat without any sacrifice of taste. Whole-wheat chapatis can be bought in specialty markets, but if not available, substitute whole-wheat tortillas.

2 large russet potatoes, baked, peeled and cubed
½ cup peas (if frozen, be sure to thaw)
1½ cups plain yogurt (divided)
2 teaspoons curry powder (or more if liked hotter)
½ teaspoon garlic powder
1 teaspoon ground cinnamon
1 tablespoon honey
¼ cup chopped fresh cilantro
6 whole-wheat chapatis
3 tablespoons melted butter or margarine

1. Combine potatoes with peas in a bowl.
2. In a separate bowl mix ¾ cup of the yogurt with curry powder, garlic powder, cinnamon and honey. Add about ¼ cup to the potato mixture.
3. Add cilantro to the remaining yogurt, cover and refrigerate.
4. Cut each chapati in half. Place 2 tablespoons of potato filling in center. Brush all edges with water to seal. Fold corners of the chapati around the filling, overlapping them to form a cone shape. Press edges together, pinching them to seal the pocket.
5. Place on a cookie sheet and brush with melted butter.
6. Bake at 375 degrees F for 15 minutes or until lightly brown and crisp. Serve with the yogurt-cilantro sauce for dipping.

Makes 1 dozen samosas.

Each samosa contains about: 156 calories, 5g protein, 22g carbohydrate, 3g fiber, 5g fat, 9mg cholesterol, 65mg sodium.

Potato Swiss Chard Soup

This soup can be served hot on a frosty evening in winter, or chilled in summer when it's too hot to cook.

1 medium onion, chopped
2 ribs celery, chopped
2 garlic cloves, minced
1 tablespoon cooking oil
4 cups cubed red potatoes
1 medium carrot, scraped, cut in chunks
1 bay leaf
5 cups vegetable stock (see page 20), or vegetable bouillon (1 teaspoon or 1 cube for each cup water)
4 cups chopped Swiss chard
¼ cup chopped fresh parsley
2 teaspoons dried thyme, crushed
½ teaspoon dried dill
½ teaspoon freshly ground black pepper
2 tablespoons sour cream

1. In a soup pot sauté onions, celery and garlic in oil until softened, about 5 minutes.
2. Add potatoes, carrot, bay leaf and stock. Bring to a boil, reduce heat and simmer for about 30 minutes.
3. Add Swiss chard, parsley, thyme and dill, and cook an additional 10 minutes. Add black pepper.
4. Remove from heat, and purée in batches in food processor.
5. If serving hot, return to soup pot and reheat about 5 minutes. If serving cold, cover and refrigerate several hours or overnight.
6. Ladle into bowls and garnish each serving with a small dollop of sour cream.

Makes 4 servings.

Each serving contains about: 209 calories, 5g protein, 36g carbohydrate, 4g fiber, 8g fat, 9mg cholesterol, 179mg sodium.

Pesto Potato Salad

The lively flavor of pesto sauce always gets steady raves, and yet before World War II this basil-cheese-oil-garlic concoction was virtually unknown outside the Genoa region of Liguria and the nearby French Riviera. Genoese sailors are said to have treasured pesto as a pungent and nostalgic reminder of their native land, and the oil in the sauce preserved it while the ships were on long voyages . The name pesto derives from the way it was made, traditionally and laboriously, with a mortar and pestle; now, of course, it's whipped together with a food processor. Incidentally, you must have freshly picked basil leaves for pesto; dried basil will never do.

Pesto Sauce (see recipe below)
8 cups cooked red potatoes, cut in chunks
1 medium red onion, sliced thin
½ cup Greek olives, pitted and halved

1. Make the pesto sauce.
2. Prepare potatoes. Put in a large bowl with onion and olives.
3. Add pesto sauce and mix till vegetables are coated. Chill thoroughly.

Pesto Sauce (makes about 2 cups)

2½ cups fresh basil, washed and stems removed
5 oz grated Parmesan cheese
⅓ cup olive oil
1 garlic clove
¼ cup walnuts or pine nuts

Put all ingredients in food processor. Purée and chill.

Makes 8 servings.

Each serving contains about: 307 calories, 11g protein, 28g carbohydrate, 3g fiber, 18g fat, 14mg cholesterol, 484mg sodium.

Potato Waffles with Onion-Mushroom Sauce

Waffles always have great appeal. Serve these as a main course for dinner —
youngsters as well as adults love them.

¾ cup mashed white potatoes
¼ cup hot milk
2 tablespoons unbleached all-purpose flour
2 tablespoons butter or margarine
2 large eggs, well beaten
Onion-Mushroom Sauce (see recipe below)

1. Whisk together potatoes, milk, flour and butter. Add eggs.
2. Spray waffle iron with vegetable cooking spray.
3. When hot, half-fill waffle iron with batter. Cook 2 to 3 minutes.
4. Repeat with remaining batter. Keep waffles warm.
5. Make Onion-Mushroom sauce, pour over waffles and serve.

Onion-Mushroom Sauce (makes about 1½ cups)

¼ cup minced onion
¼ cup chopped mushrooms
3 tablespoons butter or margarine
3 tablespoons unbleached all-purpose flour
2 vegetable bouillon cubes dissolved in 1 cup boiling water
¼ cup wine

1. In a small pan, sauté onion and mushrooms in butter for about 5 minutes. Add flour, stirring well.
2. Add bouillon mixture and wine.
3. Let sauce reach boiling, stirring constantly.

Makes 4 servings.

Each serving contains about: 262 calories, 6g protein, 17g carbohydrate, 1g fiber, 18g fat, 145mg cholesterol, 817mg sodium.

Potato and Asparagus Frittata

Potato and asparagus blend together superbly, although the frittata can be made with almost any vegetables and potato.

  1 small onion, peeled and thinly sliced
  1 small carrot, scraped and cut into 1-inch long thin julienne strips
  2 garlic cloves, minced
  1 teaspoon fresh chopped basil
  2 medium tomatoes, seeded and chopped
  2 tablespoons cooking oil (divided)
  3 small cooked Yellow Finnish or Yukon Gold potatoes
  6 to 8 asparagus spears, cooked and cut into 2-inch pieces
  ½ teaspoon freshly ground black pepper (or to taste)
  4 large whole eggs
  4 egg whites
  ⅓ cup grated Parmesan cheese

1. Sauté onion, carrot, garlic, basil and tomatoes in 1 tablespoon of the oil, until onions are translucent, about 6 to 8 minutes.
2. Add potatoes. Cook and stir until they are browned.
3. Add asparagus and cook until heated through.
4. Remove vegetables from heat, add pepper, and set aside.
5. Wipe out sauté pan and add remaining tablespoon of oil.
6. In a medium bowl, whisk together all the eggs and Parmesan cheese. Add vegetables to egg mixture and return to pan.
7. Cook over low heat until bottom of mixture is golden brown, about 5 to 8 minutes.
8. Place pan under broiler and broil about 2 minutes, until frittata is puffy and golden brown. Serve immediately.

Makes 4 servings.

Each serving contains about: 313 calories, 17g protein, 30g carbohydrate, 4g fiber, 15g fat, 219mg cholesterol, 291mg sodium.

Potato Gnocchi (Dumplings)

These gnocchi are extra special, made with the distinctive buttery-flavored yellow potatoes. Try them with your favorite marinara, pesto or Alfredo sauce, or simply sprinkled with Parmesan cheese. Irresistible!

> 4 medium Yellow Finnish or Yukon Gold potatoes, peeled and
> quartered
> 2 large eggs, well beaten
> 1½ cups unbleached all-purpose flour
> ½ teaspoon salt
> ¼ teaspoon freshly ground black pepper

1. Boil potatoes until tender, about 20 minutes. Drain well.
2. Put potatoes in food processor and purée.
3. Add eggs, flour, salt and pepper, making a firm but workable dough.
4. On a floured board, roll dough into a log shape, ¾-inch diameter. Slice into ½-inch pieces.
5. Have boiling water ready in a large pot. Drop dumplings into the boiling water a few at a time (to prevent them sticking together) for about 3 minutes. When dumplings rise to the top, remove with slotted spoon and place in serving dish.
6. Serve with your choice of sauce or Parmesan cheese.

Makes 6 servings.

Each serving contains about: 216 calories, 7g protein, 42g carbohydrate, 2g fiber, 2g fat, 71mg cholesterol, 204mg sodium.

Potato Kugel Pudding

When Sandra was a child, this savory potato kugel was always made for a celebration or holiday and usually signaled a happy occasion. Kugel is a tradional dish among Eastern European Jews. Matzo meal can be found in the ethnic section of most supermarkets.

> 6 large russet potatoes, peeled
> 1 medium onion, grated
> 3 large eggs, well beaten
> 4 tablespoons matzo meal or cracker meal
> 1 teaspoon baking powder
> 1 teaspoon salt
> ½ teaspoon freshly ground black pepper
> 4 tablespoons butter or margarine, melted (divided)

1. Grate potatoes with the grater blade of a food processor or by hand.
2. In a large bowl mix potatoes with all other ingredients except 2 tablespoons of the butter.
3. Spray or grease a 1½-quart baking pan and pour in mixture. Pour remaining 2 tablespoons butter on top.
4. Bake at 350 degrees F for 1 hour, or until mixture is set and lightly browned. Serve hot.

Makes 4 to 5 servings.

Each serving contains about: 381 calories, 10g protein, 52g carbohydrate, 4g fiber, 16g fat, 190mg cholesterol, 791mg sodium.

Posh Potatoes with Capers

When selecting capers, the immature buds of the caper bush, connoisseurs prefer the smallest variety called nonpareils.

    7 medium-size Yellow Finnish or Yukon Gold potatoes
    1 shallot, finely chopped
    1 garlic clove, crushed
    3 tablespoons olive oil
    2 tablespoons unbleached all-purpose flour
    1¼ cups vegetable stock (see page 20), or vegetable bouillon (1 teaspoon
        or 1 cube for each cup water)
    2 teaspoons capers, rinsed and drained
    1 teaspoon salt
    ¼ teaspoon freshly ground black pepper

1. Cook potatoes in microwave until tender. Remove skins and cut each potato into 2 or 3 pieces. Keep warm.
2. Cook shallot and garlic in olive oil for about 5 minutes or until soft. Add flour and stir for 2 minutes.
3. Add stock, capers, salt and pepper, and cook until thickened, about 20 minutes.
4. Place potatoes in serving dish. Pour caper sauce over potatoes to coat well. Serve hot.

Makes 4 servings.

Each serving contains about: 396 calories, 7g protein, 70g carbohydrate, 4g fiber, 11g fat, 0mg cholesterol, 588mg sodium.

Potato Garlic Sauce

This versatile sauce can be served either hot or cold. When hot, it's great on fresh steamed vegetables; served chilled, it makes a creamy dip for crisp cold sticks of celery, carrots, jicama and cauliflowerets.

1 cup mashed cooked white potatoes
4 medium garlic cloves
½ cup commercial mayonnaise
½ cup chopped pine nuts or walnuts
¼ cup water
1 teaspoon rice vinegar

1. Put all ingredients in food processor and blend until smooth.
2. For a hot sauce, pour into a small pan and place over low heat until heated through.
3. For a cold dipping sauce, cover and chill in the refrigerator for several hours or overnight.

Makes 2 cups, about 6 servings.

Each serving contains about: 226 calories, 2g protein, 9g carbohydrate, 1g fiber, 21g fat, 11mg cholesterol, 212mg sodium.

R

Radish

(*Raphanus sativus*)　　See also its cousin, Daikon.

History and lore: The word radish comes from the Latin *radix* meaning "root."

The radish has probably been cultivated since Neolithic times. No one is certain of its origin because its wild ancestor has disappeared, but the radish is believed to have come from the Far East since there are many Asian varieties and the Chinese have made the greatest use of this plant — not only the root, but also the leaves, pods and seeds.

Ancient Egyptians were growing it to produce radish-seed oil long before they acquired the olive; Pliny complained about farmers who stopped growing grain because they preferred to sow larger quantities of oil-radishes that fetched higher prices and were more profitable.

The Ancient Greeks valued radishes highly: when making offerings to their gods of esteemed vegetables, they would present replicas of these foods modeled in metal: beets in silver, turnips in lead and radishes in gold. Even today, the Japanese wrap and present radishes as honorable gifts for hosts and friends, and the Chinese consider the carving of radishes into intricate flower shapes is an art-form.

The black radish (*R.sativus*, var. *niger*) is also believed to have come from China. This one is in the family of winter-radishes that can be kept longer, originally grown for winter storage. It was favored centuries ago in European folk medicine as a powerful ingredient in potions to cure warts, insanity and detect the presence of witches!

147

Seasons when available: Red radishes are in supermarkets year-round. Black radishes are available primarily in the winter, although some markets may have them all year.

What to look for when shopping: Shop for smooth, firm red radishes with a minimum of surface pits. Avoid any with black spots and pits, or any that are cracked, spongy, flabby or wilted. Check if leaves are intact, as their greenness can indicate root freshness.

Black radishes look more like black turnips, with white flesh and stronger turnip-like flavor. Unlike red radishes, they maintain their skin color during cooking.

Asian markets and farmers' markets often sell interesting Oriental varieties with skins of green, pink, purple, black and white, and flesh of pink, red or white.

Nutritional highlights: Low in calories and sodium; some vitamin C and calcium.

Amount for 4 servings: A cello-wrapped bag or about 1 lb.

How to store: Remove leaves. Store in plastic bags in the refrigerator. Use red radishes promptly, as long storage makes them flabby and hollow-centered. Do not freeze. Keep black radishes wrapped in plastic and refrigerated; they can keep for a month or so during which time their flavor will mellow.

Basic prep: All radishes need a good scrub before use, and a trimming of leafy tops and tails. Red radishes are always left unpeeled, as we enjoy them for their color. Whether or not to peel black radishes depends on the toughness of the skin and the dish you are preparing. Stripe-peeling of black radishes with a lemon zester leaves stunning designs of black and white.

All radishes enjoy a dip in an ice-water bath before serving, to enhance crispness. If serving black radishes raw and you want to tame some of the strong flavor, they need salting for an hour or longer: toss 1 teaspoon salt with about 1 cup of shredded, chopped or sliced black radish in a small bowl; cover with plastic and set aside. Rinse, press out all liquid and blot dry before serving.

Ways to serve: Radishes make attractive colorful appetizers, carved into decorative shapes and served well-chilled. Slice thinly or grate in salads and salsas.

East European or Jewish families enjoy black radish coarsely grated, salted, and rinsed, then tossed with sour cream, and served with pumpernickel bread.

Cook black radishes as you would turnips: steamed or boiled (about 20 minutes), puréed, served in a cream sauce. Or diced and added to stir-fries and stews.

———————

Radish Licorice Soup

Ground anise gives this soup the deliciously different flavor of licorice, and offers an innovative way to serve radishes.

    4 tablespoons butter or margarine (divided)
    7 cups sliced radishes
    ½ cup chopped onion
    ½ cup chopped celery
    4 tablespoons cornstarch
    3 cups milk
    2 teaspoons ground anise
    Salt and pepper to taste

1. Melt 2 tablespoons of butter in a soup pot and sauté radishes, onion and celery till translucent, about 4 minutes. Set aside.
2. In another pan, melt remaining 2 tablespoons butter, add cornstarch and blend to a smooth paste. Add milk a little at a time, stirring until smooth and thickened.
3. Blend vegetables in food processor and purée.
4. Combine puréed vegetables and sauce back in soup pot. Add ground anise, salt and pepper. Reheat and serve warm.

Makes 6 servings.

Each serving contains about: 187 calories, 5g protein, 16g carbohydrate, 3g fiber, 12g fat, 37mg cholesterol, 261mg sodium.

Radish Stuffed Tomatoes

The filling, prepared in the food processor, can be made in minutes. A great luncheon dish.

4 medium tomatoes, centers removed
3 large radishes, cut in quarters
½ small cucumber, cut in pieces
1 small onion, cut in pieces
½ small green bell pepper, cut in pieces
1 lb creamed cottage cheese
½ teaspoon dry mustard
½ teaspoon celery salt
⅛ teaspoon freshly ground black pepper
Chopped parsley for garnish (optional)

1. Remove tops from tomatoes and scoop out center pulp. Set aside tomatoes to drain well.
2. Put in food processor, radishes, cucumber, onion and green bell pepper. Process until a chopped consistency.
3. Add cottage cheese, mustard, celery salt and black pepper. Process until chunky and well mixed.
4. Fill tomatoes with mixture, sprinkle with chopped parsley, and serve well chilled.

Makes 4 servings.

Each serving contains about: 159 calories, 16g protein, 12g carbohydrate, 3g fiber, 6g fat, 17mg cholesterol, 614mg sodium.

Spicy Radish Relish

Here's a relish that's good with any raw veggies. It also makes a delicious spread on pumpernickel or any dark bread. Italian Seasoning can be found in most supermarkets.

> 1 (15-oz) can diced or crushed tomatoes
> 1 cup chopped onion
> 2 garlic cloves, minced
> 2 teaspoons ground cumin
> 1 tablespoon chili powder
> 1 tablespoon Italian Seasoning (or dried basil)
> 1 tablespoon chopped fresh parsley
> 2 cups sliced red radishes

1. In a medium pan gently simmer all ingredients except radishes over low heat for about 20 minutes.
2. Pour over radishes and serve well chilled.

Makes 6 servings.

Each serving contains about: 39 calories, 2g protein, 8g carbohydrate, 2g fiber, 1g fat, 0mg cholesterol, 31mg sodium.

Rutabaga

(Brassica napobrassica)   See also its cousin, Turnip.

Also known as: Swedish turnip; Swedes; Russian turnip.

History and lore: The word rutabaga comes from the Swedish *rotabagge*, "baggy root." A botanist developed rutabagas in the 17th century, by cross-breeding a turnip with a cabbage, making it a relative of kohlrabi. Since Swedish people grow a lot of rutabagas, they came to be called Swedish turnips or Swedes. They are grown extensively in Northern Europe, Britain and Canada, and to a lesser extent in the U.S.

They were among the first vegetables grown by colonizers in America, especially settlers from Scandinavian countries, as they farmed new lands, because the roots helped to break up poor soils. Supplies today come mainly from Wisconsin and Minnesota, and especially from Canada.

Seasons when available: They are basically a cool-weather crop, with greater quantities available between October and February.

What to look for when shopping: Look for smooth roots that are heavy, well-shaped (round or elongated), and firm — not soft or wrinkled. They are often waxed to prevent dehydration. The yellow-orange skin of rutabagas is pigmented with purple streaks on the top half because they grow half out of the soil. The flavor is mild and turnip-like.

Nutritional highlights: Low in calories; a healthy source of potassium and vitamins A and C. The rutabaga is one of the cruciferous vegetables believed to be a cancer preventive.

Amount for 4 servings: 1 large or 2 medium (about 1 lb).

How to store: Keep in a paper sack or airy basket at room temperature for up to 1 week. Or refrigerate, wrapped in plastic, for up to 1 month.

Basic prep: Scrub roots well. If they have been preserved with wax, remove the coating with a sharp knife. For maximum nutrition, cook rutabagas unpeeled; for more elegant presentation, pare skin with a vegetable peeler to remove the thinnest possible layer. Cut into 2-inch pieces.

For boiling, cook rutabaga chunks in 1-inch boiling water for 20 to 30 minutes, or until tender. Drain well.

Ways to serve: Mashed, baked, grated into fritter batter or added to stews. Make a beautiful soup by thinning mashed rutabagas with milk; or whisk eggs into the mash and bake, for a fluffy pudding.

Bashed neeps, a dish "fit for a Queen," is a Scottish specialty: Diced and simmered roots are mashed and seasoned with salt, pepper, nutmeg, butter and cream.

Rutabaga Chips

Rutabagas have a mellow flavor and good texture for making quick appetizing snacks. Slice them into various shapes to give eye-catching appeal. Serve with small bowls of spicy ketchup or zesty cream-style horseradish, or sprinkle paprika or cayenne pepper for added zip.

> 1 large rutabaga, about 1 lb, thinly peeled
> Oil for frying (about 1 cup)
> Salt and pepper to taste

1. Scrub rutabaga and blot thoroughly dry with a paper towel.
2. Slice across the grain into ⅛-inch thick circles and slice each circle in half.
3. Heat cooking oil until hot (not smoking). Place a single layer of slices in oil, but do not crowd the pan.
4. Fry roots until golden brown, stirring and turning occasionally to improve browning. Remove slices with a slotted spoon, drain on paper towel and keep warm.
5. Sprinkle with salt and pepper, and serve immediately with bowls of dipping sauces or extra seasoning.

Makes 4 servings.

Each serving contains about: 186 calories, 1g protein, 9g carbohydrate, 2g fiber, 17g fat, 0mg cholesterol, 156mg sodium.

Rutabaga Vegetable Pâté

Colorfully layered pâté can be the perfect centerpiece for a buffet party, easy to make the day before, leaving you free to enjoy the company of your friends. When shopping for rutabagas, choose small ones with their more delicate flavor.

2 or 3 small rutabagas (about 1 lb), peeled and cut into 2-inch pieces
3 large eggs
¼ cup heavy cream
4 medium carrots, sliced
4 leeks, cleaned, trimmed and sliced
⅓ lb green beans, cut in small pieces
3 small turnips, peeled and quartered
2 (10-oz) packages frozen chopped spinach, thawed and drained
1 tablespoon dried thyme
2 teaspoons dried basil
1 teaspoon garlic powder
⅓ cup bread crumbs

1. Cook rutabaga in boiling water about 20 minutes or until tender. Drain and purée in food processor. Beat eggs and cream together and add to rutabaga purée.
2. Microwave carrots, leeks, green beans and turnips in separate dishes, for about 5 minutes on HIGH or until tender. Purée each vegetable.
3. Line up the six bowls including rutabaga and spinach. Season the carrot and turnip purées with thyme, season green beans and leeks with basil, and season spinach with garlic powder.
4. Lightly coat a 9 x 5-inch loaf pan with nonstick cooking spray and sprinkle bottom with bread crumbs.
5. Cover bread crumbs with about one-third spinach purée. Layer spinach with rutabaga purée, then carrot over rutabaga. Continue alternating vegetable layers.
6. Cover pâté with foil and slit center of foil for steam to escape. Then place loaf pan in a larger pan with hot water about 2 inches up the sides.
7. Bake at 400 degrees F for 30 minutes. Cool at room temperature for about 2 hours.
8. Refrigerate until well chilled, unmold on a serving platter and slice.

Makes one 9 x 5-inch loaf, about 12 servings.

Each serving contains about: 116 calories, 5g protein, 18g carbohydrate, 4g fiber, 4g fat, 60mg cholesterol, 117mg sodium.

Southwest Rutabagas

Rutabagas become a zesty Southwest-style main dish when stuffed with beans and spicy seasonings.

4 rutabagas (about 2 lbs), peeled
½ medium onion, minced
1 tablespoon canola oil
1 (16-oz) can pinto beans, drained and rinsed
1 teaspoon chili powder
½ teaspoon ground cumin
½ teaspoon garlic powder
⅛ teaspoon cayenne pepper
½ cup chopped parsley for garnish

1. Scoop out centers of rutabagas and slice off a piece from bottoms so vegetables will stand. Cook in boiling water for 20 to 30 minutes until tender.
2. Sauté onion in oil until translucent. Add beans, chili powder, cumin, garlic powder and cayenne. Cook and stir until well blended.
3. Lightly spoon bean mixture into centers of rutabagas.
4. Garnish with chopped parsley, and serve hot.

Makes 4 servings.

Each serving contains about: 222 calories, 9g protein, 39g carbohydrate, 5g fiber, 4g fat, 0mg cholesterol, 442mg sodium.

Savory Rutabaga Cake

This "cake" was served to us as a side dish one evening at a dinner party with friends. It was so good and simple, we told our hostess we weren't leaving until we had the recipe!

> 4 cups grated rutabagas
> 2 cups grated potatoes
> ½ cup grated onion
> 1 garlic clove, minced
> 4 tablespoons olive oil (divided)
> 1 teaspoon seasoned salt

1. Toss together rutabagas, potatoes, onion and garlic.
2. Heat 2 tablespoons of the oil in a cast-iron skillet or heavy nonstick frying pan. Spoon in the vegetable mixture, flattening it evenly in the pan. Sprinkle with seasoned salt.
3. Turn down the heat, cover and cook till bottom is nicely brown, about 10 to 15 minutes.
4. To turn the cake, slip it out of the pan onto a plate. Place another plate on top of the cake and invert it.
5. Add remaining oil to pan, and return cake to cook and brown the second side.
6. Slice into wedges and serve hot.

Makes 6 servings.

Each serving contains about: 158 calories, 2g protein, 18g carbohydrate, 2g fiber, 9g fat, 0mg cholesterol, 377mg sodium.

Quick Apple-Butter Rutabagas

Select small rutabagas for their sweeter taste. Served as a sweet side dish, the flavor is similar to a spicy baked apple, with the nuts giving a crunchy texture.

3 cups (about 1lb) rutabagas, peeled and chopped
1 large apple (such as a sweet Delicious), peeled and chopped
2 tablespoons butter or margarine
⅓ cup brown sugar
¼ teaspoon ground allspice
¼ teaspoon ground cinnamon
¼ teaspoon ground nutmeg
¼ cup chopped pecans or walnuts

1. Microwave rutabagas in a glass dish with ¼ cup water, on HIGH for about 12 to 15 minutes till tender. Drain.
2. Microwave apple and butter on HIGH for about 2 minutes.
3. Add all ingredients to rutabagas, stirring well until sugar melts.
4. Mix in chopped nuts, and serve.

Makes 4 servings.

Each serving contains about: 222 calories, 2g protein, 32g carbohydrate, 3g fiber, 11g fat, 15mg cholesterol, 85mg sodium.

S

Salsify

(Tragopogon porrifolius)

Also known as: White salsify; Oyster plant; Vegetable oyster; Purple goat's beard. Black salsify (*Scorzonera Hispanica*) from an unrelated species, is also known as scorzoner.

History and lore: Salsify seems to have been native to the Mediterranean where it was probably gathered by the ancient Egyptians. It still grows wild around European villages. Thomas Jefferson is said to have planted more of this vegetable than other crops we now consider common.

Another name for black salsify is viper grass, because people of the Iberian peninsula believed the plant's juices were an antidote to snakebite. (*Escorço* is Catalan for viper.)

Seasons when available: Fall, winter and spring (roughly October through April), and occasionally during summer.

What to look for when shopping: Roots should be firm and smooth, with tan-colored skins like twisted parsnips, and covered with tiny rootlets. Flesh is off-white, with a flavor delicately similar to oysters, hence the alternative name.

Black salsify (black oyster plant), with extremely thin tapered roots and a dark brown skin, may be found in specialty stores. Supplies, generally imported from Europe, are limited.

Nutritional highlights: Low in calories and sodium, high in potassium.

Amount for 4 servings: About 1 lb, usually sold in a cello bag.

How to store: Wrap tightly in plastic and refrigerate, for up to 2 weeks.

Basic prep: Scrub well. Salsify darkens when the root is cut. Cook it immediately; or drop it in a bowl of water with 2 tablespoons vinegar or lemon juice and let stand 10 minutes, to prevent darkening. Boil them with skins intact, and the skins slip off after a slight cooking.

As with rutabagas and turnips, salsify can cause flatulence. Go easy on portions the first time, to test your digestive system. The problem can be remedied with a little Beano or Be Sure; see directions on packages.

Ways to serve: Braise chunks in a dab of butter and vegetable broth, for a delicate flavor, or serve with a cheese sauce. Boil, steam, purée for soups and chowders, or bake as a scalloped dish with layers of oyster crackers.

Wine-Marinated Salsify

These tasty morsels can be served as appetizers or as a side dish.

1½ to 2 lbs salsify, peeled and cut into 2-inch pieces
1 tablespoon butter or margarine
1 tablespoon fresh lemon juice
½ cup white wine
Seasoned flour:
     ½ cup unbleached all-purpose flour
     1 teaspoon salt
     1 teaspoon freshly ground black pepper
     ½ teaspoon ground paprika (preferably Hungarian)
Oil for frying (about 1 cup)

1. Place salsify in pot and barely cover with water. Add butter and lemon juice. Simmer for about 45 minutes or until salsify is tender. Drain.
2. Sprinkle wine over salsify and let sit for about 1 hour. Drain.
3. Prepare seasoned flour in a separate bowl, mixing flour, salt, pepper and paprika.
4. Heat oil in pan. Dip each piece of salsify in flour mixture and then into the hot oil, frying till golden brown. Drain well on paper towel.

Makes 4 servings.

Each serving contains about: 365 calories, 6g protein, 39g carbohydrate, 4g fiber, 20g fat, 8mg cholesterol, 591mg sodium.

Salsify Salad

The mock-Hollandaise sauce accents the asparagus-like flavor of the salsify.
Serve this salad warm or at room temperature with a pasta main dish, and a
crisp green salad to complete the meal.

2 lbs salsify
½ cup butter or margarine
3 egg yolks
2 tablespoons fresh lemon juice
Salt and pepper to taste
¼ cup chopped black olives
½ cup chopped fresh parsley

1. Peel salsify and remove top and bottom. Cut roots into bite size pieces, and put into a pot of boiling water for about 10 minutes, until they soften.
2. Rinse in cold water and drain.
3. Melt butter until very hot. Place egg yolks and lemon juice in food processor, adding melted butter very slowly, letting the yolks absorb the butter. Season with salt and pepper.
4. Pour over salsify and garnish with black olives and parsley.

Makes 6 servings.

Each serving contains about: 281 calories, 6g protein, 25g carbohydrate, 4g fiber, 19g fat, 147mg cholesterol, 353mg sodium.

Salsify with Red Peppers

Red peppers, mushrooms and Oriental seasoning go beautifully with the flavor of salsify. Serve on a bed of rice for a main dish.

Canned straw mushrooms are sold in Oriental grocers. If difficult to obtain, use regular canned mushrooms. Mock-chicken bouillon powder, found in health-food stores and specialty markets, is usually sold loose, by the pound. Use 1 teaspoon for each cup water.

2 lbs salsify, peeled and cut into 2-inch pieces
4 cups mock-chicken stock
2 tablespoons peanut or vegetable oil
2 garlic cloves, crushed
2 red bell peppers, seeded and sliced
1 (15-oz) can straw mushrooms, drained and rinsed
1 tablespoon soy sauce
½ cup chopped scallions (optional garnish)

1. Boil salsify in mock-chicken stock for 10 to 15 minutes, until tender. Drain, reserving liquid.
2. In a pan, heat oil with garlic. Add peppers, mushrooms and salsify, and sauté for about 5 minutes. If getting dry, add some reserved liquid. Add soy sauce, and heat for another minute until well blended.
3. Remove from heat and sprinkle with chopped scallions.

Makes 4 servings.

Each serving contains about: 270 calories, 10g protein, 44g carbohydrate, 8g fiber, 8g fat, 0mg cholesterol, 1868mg sodium.

Scallion

(*Allium* genus)   See also its cousins: Onion, Leek, Garlic, Shallot.

Also known as: Green onion; Spring onion; Bunching onion. Similar variety: Knob onion.

History and lore: The word scallion comes, via Middle English *scaloun*, from Latin *Ascalon*, an ancient trading port (Ashqelon) in the Levant particularly associated with this member of the onion family.

Seasons when available: All year.

What to look for when shopping: Look for crisp green tops, with 2 to 3 inches of white stem and a round bulbous root; sold in bunches of about 6 stalks. White stem has milder flavor than green tops.

Knob onions are mature scallions with enlarged bulbs, and usually sold in bunches of only 4 stalks.

Nutritional highlights: Low in calories and sodium; high in potassium.

Amount for 4 servings: 1 or 2 bunches.

How to store: Wipe with damp paper towel, seal in plastic bag and refrigerate. Best used in 4 or 5 days but may keep up to 2 weeks.

Basic prep: Trim off limp tops and any slimy layers. Chop or slice tender green tops, white stems and bulbs for eating raw in salads, salsas, appetizers, and as garnishes for soups and side dishes. They can be added to stir-fries, scrambled eggs, pilafs and scalloped dishes. They can substitute for leeks.

Ways to serve: Cook scallions in 1-inch boiling water for about 10 minutes, or until tender. Serve with melted butter, salt and pepper, or a sprinkle of Parmesan.

Scallion Eggrolls

Eggroll skins can be found in most supermarkets. For best results, make the appetizers immediately before serving, as rolling them ahead of time can sometimes cause the skins to split. Dip the eggrolls in hot mustard, Chinese sweet sauce or soy sauce for a great taste.

1 bunch scallions, washed, cleaned and finely chopped
½ lb fresh mushrooms, washed and finely chopped
½ cup finely grated carrots
1½ cups finely diced celery
1 (8-oz) can water chestnuts, drained and chopped
½ small head Bok Choy cabbage (or regular cabbage), cleaned and grated
½ lb fresh bean sprouts, washed and drained
¼ cup peanut butter
1 (1-lb) package eggroll skins
Oil for frying (about 1 cup)

1. Mix all ingredients, except eggroll skins and oil, together in a large mixing bowl.
2. Heat oil, deep enough to brown one side of each eggroll at a time.
3. Fill eggroll skin with about 2 tablespoons of vegetables in center. Tuck in both sides as you roll, and seal with water.
4. Place in hot oil till brown on one side, then turn over to other side to finish browning.
5. Drain well on paper towels and serve hot.

Makes approximately 10 eggrolls.

Each eggroll contains about: 264 calories, 8g protein, 37g carbohydrate, 5g fiber, 10g fat, 5mg cholesterol, 176mg sodium.

Scallion-Stuffed Mushrooms

These are easy hors d'oeuvres to make in the microwave. Make plenty as they go fast!

¼ cup minced scallions
2 tablespoons minced green bell pepper
2 garlic cloves, minced
4 tablespoons butter or margarine (divided)
½ teaspoon Worcestershire sauce
1 (3-oz) package cream cheese, at room temperature
1 lb small fresh mushrooms, washed and dried, stems separated
¾ cup bread crumbs

1. Mix scallions, bell pepper and garlic with 2 tablespoons of the butter. Put in glass bowl, cover and microwave on HIGH for 4 minutes, stirring once.
2. Mix in Worcestershire sauce and cream cheese. Chop mushroom stems and add to scallion mixture, then spoon mixture into mushroom centers.
3. Heat bread crumbs and remaining butter in microwave on HIGH for 1 minute. Stir well.
4. Press buttered crumbs on top of stuffed mushrooms. Place mushrooms on a glass baking dish, filling-side up. Cook in microwave on HIGH for 2 minutes.
5. Repeat till all mushrooms are cooked. Serve hot.

Makes about 35 appetizers.

Each appetizer contains about: 32 calories, 1g protein, 2g carbohydrate, 1g fiber, 2g fat, 6mg cholesterol, 38mg sodium.

Scallion Pie

If you're short of time, bake the filling in a greased pan as you would a custard, without bothering with the pastry shell, and spoon it from the baking dish.

   Pastry for a 9-inch pie shell (see recipe below)
   3 tablespoons butter or margarine
   3 cups sliced scallions
   2 large eggs, slightly beaten
   ½ cup light cream or canned evaporated milk
   1 teaspoon salt
   ½ teaspoon freshly ground black pepper
   ¼ teaspoon ground nutmeg

1. Make pastry.
2. Melt butter in a small saucepan and cook scallions slowly until tender. Spoon scallions into unbaked pie shell.
3. In a small bowl whisk eggs with cream, salt, pepper and nutmeg, and pour over scallions.
4. Bake at 425 degrees F until filling is firm, about 20 minutes.

Pastry (for one single-crust 9-inch pie)

   ½ cup (1 stick) margarine
   1 teaspoon granulated sugar
   ⅛ teaspoon salt
   1¼ cups unbleached all-purpose or pastry flour
   2 tablespoons ice water

Mix all ingredients. Chill in freezer for about ½ hour. Roll out and trim to fit 9-inch pie pan, giving edges a decorative finish with fingertips.

Makes one 9-inch pie, about 8 servings.

Each serving contains about: 288 calories, 5g protein, 19g carbohydrate, 1g fiber, 22g fat, 81mg cholesterol, 524mg sodium.

Jill's Skinny Scallion Crackers

Sandra's daughter Jill loves crackers but doesn't like fat, so she devised these crisp munchies to satisfy her cravings during her last pregnancy. The crackers become crisp while cooling.

1½ cups chopped scallions
2 cups whole-wheat flour
½ cup wheat germ
1½ teaspoons baking powder
1 (8-oz) package fat-free cream cheese
5 tablespoons water
1 egg white

1. Spray a pan with nonstick cooking spray and sauté scallions till limp, about 4 minutes.
2. Put dry ingredients and cream cheese in a food processor. Add water and scallions and put on pulse action until dough forms a ball. Remove and chill for about 1½ hours.
3. Roll out dough and cut into circles with a cookie cutter. Transfer to a sprayed cookie sheet and pierce each cracker several times with a fork. Brush crackers with egg white.
4. Bake at 375 degrees F for 25 to 30 minutes until golden brown. Cool on wire rack.

Makes about 36 crackers.

Each cracker contains about: 36 calories, 2g protein, 6g carbohydrate, 1g fiber, 1g fat, 1mg cholesterol, 47mg sodium.

Shallot

(Allium aggregatum)

Also known as: Echalote.

History and lore: The name shallot comes, via French *eschalot*, from Latin *Ascalon*, the name of an ancient trading port (Ashqelon) in the Levant particularly associated with this gourmet member of the onion family. This root is said to have originated in the Eastern Mediterranean, Syria or the Holy Land, and the French probably introduced it to Europe in the Early Christian era.

Seasons when available: Year-round.

What to look for when shopping: They most closely resemble large separated garlic cloves, oval in shape with reddish brown or purplish papery skins. Select firm bulbs with no soft or moldy areas. The tender white flesh and lovely mild garlic-onion flavor are considered easier to digest than garlic or onions.

Nutritional highlights: Low in calories and sodium; a good source of potassium, iron and calcium.

Amount for 4 servings: Often sold in small baskets or cello bags containing about 4 oz.

How to store: Don't refrigerate, as they will absorb moisture and develop molds. Keep in a paper sack or airy vegetable basket in a cool dry place, for up to 3 weeks. For longer storage, peel bulbs, cover with white wine in a screw-top jar, and refrigerate.

Basic prep: Peel a shallot as you would an ordinary fresh onion, trimming off dry roots and pulling off the papery layer. Then chop, mince or slice thinly.

Ways to serve: Use in dishes needing onions or garlic: salads, cream sauces, sautés, braises, casseroles, egg dishes, stews, stir-fries, or glazed with butter, sugar and tarragon vinegar.

Shallot, Spinach and Noodle Casserole

Sandra's Russian background is evident with this hearty casserole from the Ukraine.

6 tablespoons butter or margarine (divided)
3 cups cooked noodles, well drained (follow directions on package)
¾ cup grated Swiss cheese (divided)
1 cup peeled and chopped shallots
4 (10-oz) packages frozen chopped spinach, squeezed and drained
½ teaspoon freshly ground nutmeg
¼ teaspoon freshly ground black pepper
½ cup bread crumbs
3 hard-boiled eggs, quartered (optional)

1. Melt 2 tablespoons of the butter and toss with noodles and ½ cup of cheese. Set aside.
2. In a large skillet, sauté shallots in 2 more tablespoons butter for about 5 minutes or until soft.
3. Stir in spinach and cook until all moisture is gone. Add nutmeg and black pepper. Set aside.
4. Coat the bottom of a 2-quart baking dish with vegetable cooking spray.
5. Layer one-third noodles on bottom of dish; top with one-half shallot-spinach mixture. Repeat layering, ending with noodles.
6. Melt last 2 tablespoons butter, and stir in bread crumbs and remaining ¼ cup cheese. Sprinkle crumb-cheese topping on casserole.
7. Bake at 350 degrees F for about 30 minutes, or until the topping is golden brown.
8. Garnish with hard-boiled eggs, if desired.

Makes 6 servings.

Each serving contains about: 367 calories, 16g protein, 41g carbohydrate, 7g fiber, 17g fat, 71mg cholesterol, 386mg sodium.

Show-Off Shallots

Shallots in a simple cream sauce is a lovely way to appreciate their subtle distinctive flavor.

1 lb small firm shallots, peeled and halved
4 tablespoons butter or margarine (divided)
2 tablespoons unbleached all-purpose flour
½ teaspoon salt
¼ teaspoon freshly ground black pepper
1 cup light cream
Chopped parsley for garnish (optional)

1. Sauté shallots in 2 tablespoons of the butter for about 12 to 15 minutes, or until tender.
2. In a separate pan melt remaining butter, add flour, salt and pepper and stir till bubbly. Remove from heat. Stir in cream then cook gently, stirring constantly, for about 1 minute. Pour over shallots.
3. Garnish with chopped parsley, if desired.

Makes 4 servings.

Each serving contains about: 372 calories, 5g protein, 24g carbohydrate, 1g fiber, 30g fat, 97mg cholesterol, 418mg sodium.

Sweet and Sour Shallots

A side dish that not only tastes delicious but looks attractive.

¼ cup golden raisins
⅓ cup Marsala wine or Sherry
1 lb shallots, peeled
4 tablespoons canola oil
2 teaspoons tomato paste
1 tablespoon red-wine vinegar
1½ teaspoons granulated sugar
2 tablespoons water
¼ cup chopped pine nuts or walnuts

1. Soak raisins in wine for about 10 minutes. Set aside.
2. Brown shallots in oil.
3. Drain raisins and add wine to shallots, along with tomato paste, red-wine vinegar, sugar and water. Simmer on low heat for about 10 minutes.
4. Add raisins and nuts, and simmer another 25 minutes, or until shallots are tender and sauce is reduced to a rich glaze.

Makes 4 servings.

Each serving contains about: 314 calories, 4g protein, 31g carbohydrate, 2g fiber, 18g fat, 0mg cholesterol, 19mg sodium.

Shallot-Butter Garlic Bread

This bread is easy to make, its brown topping looks appetizing, and the loaf will give your home the inviting fragrance of a trattoria!

>   2 tablespoons olive oil
>   1 stick (½ cup) butter or margarine
>   3 tablespoons finely chopped shallots
>   4 large garlic cloves, minced
>   2 tablespoons oregano
>   1 (1 lb) loaf French bread
>   ½ cup freshly grated Parmesan cheese

1. Heat olive oil and butter in a small pan. Add shallots, garlic and oregano, and simmer until shallots are tender.
2. Slice bread lengthwise into two long halves. With a pastry brush, spread shallot mixture onto the bread until well covered. Sprinkle with Parmesan cheese.
3. Bake at 350 degrees F for about 15 minutes, or until brown and bubbly.

Makes one French loaf, about 16 slices.

Each slice contains about: 160 calories, 4g protein, 15g carbohydrate, 1g fiber, 9g fat, 18mg cholesterol, 264mg sodium.

Sweet potato

(Ipomea batatas)   See also Boniato.

Also known as: Jersey sweet; "Yam."

History and lore: We mustn't confuse the sweet potato (which is in the morning-glory family) with the common white potato or with the tropical yam, as they are entirely unrelated. The true yam of African origin is grown in the tropics, and is not available in the United States except in ethnic markets.

Archeologists have found the oldest remains of the sweet potato in Peru where it has been grown since 750 B.C. When Christopher Columbus first came to America, he saw many varieties of sweet potato, and was served four kinds at a feast given in his honor by the island-king on St. Thomas in the Caribbean. In the Arawak language the vegetable was known as *batatas*, out of which came the word potato.

At the end of the 15th century when Spaniards took the vegetable back to Spain, it was immediately received with enthusiasm (unlike the initial opposition to the white potato), and it went into general cultivation. From Spain, the root traveled to England where it was known as the "Spanish potato"; King Henry VIII ate them in a sweet spiced pie which he is said to have appreciated greatly. In 1589, the English explorer Richard Hakluyt wrote: *These potatoes be the most delicate rootes that may be eaten, and doe farre exceed our passeneps or carets.*

The Spaniards also spread the cultivation of the sweet potato to the Philippines and other islands in the Pacific, where it became a dietary staple. The tubers are now widely grown in warmer climates around the world.

Seasons when available: All year, but peak supply and best quality arrive in markets from October to January.

What to look for when shopping: Choose rock-hard tubers with tapered ends; uniform thickness will ensure even cooking. Avoid any with cuts, or soft moldy spots. Sweet potatoes fall into one of two broad categories: the

Puerto Rico, which is orange-fleshed, very sweet, dense and moist; and the New Jersey, which is paler, starchier and less sugary. Deeper colors have more beta-carotene.

Nutritional highlights: A good source of beta-carotene, hence vitamin A; some vitamin C and potassium, and a little calcium and iron.

Amount for 4 servings: Four medium size (1 to 1¼ lbs) Don't buy more than you can use promptly.

How to store: Because of a high moisture content, sweet potatoes are more perishable than whites. Store them in an airy basket or open paper sack (not plastic) in a cool dry dark place, but not the refrigerator where they will quickly spoil. Use within a week or 10 days.

Basic prep: Scrub them gently with a soft brush under cold running water, then boil, steam, sauté in butter, grill, roast, mash or purée. Add to delicious fritters, fluffy soufflés, soups and stews for a sweet accent, or toss into muffins, quick breads and dessert pies.

To boil, cut into 2-inch chunks, cover with boiling water and cook about 20 minutes. Drain well and slip off skins. Serve whole, or mash with a little butter, salt and pepper.

Bake unpeeled sweet potatoes at 375 degrees F until soft, about 50 minutes.

To make splendid sweet potato "chips," drizzle thin slices with melted butter on a lightly oiled baking sheet, and broil for 5 minutes.

Ways to serve: Tradition dictates that sweet potatoes be topped with brown sugar, honey or marshmallows, duplicating the tubers' natural sweetness. A better idea is to whip them with a dash of orange juice or dry Sherry and a sprinkle of nutmeg, or a dollop of plain yogurt. Aromatic partners for sweet potatoes are herbs such as cilantro, rosemary and thyme, and they pair nicely with white wine, cider, lemon or orange juice.

For a heart-healthy spread: purée cooked sweet potato and grated carrot, season with garlic, black pepper and a bit of olive oil; serve on toast instead of butter or margarine.

Indian Sweet Potato Soup

A beautiful blend of sweet potatoes and curry gives this soup a delicate touch. The Indian spice, garam masala, *can be bought in some health-food stores, Oriental or specialty stores.*

1 cup chopped onion
2 tablespoons butter or margarine
8 cups cubed sweet potatoes
1 cup water
1 teaspoon curry powder
1 teaspoon *garam masala* (or 2 more teaspoons curry)
2 cups milk
2 cups half-and-half
Salt and pepper to taste
Chopped parsley (optional)

1. In a soup pot sauté onion in butter until limp, about 4 minutes.
2. Add sweet potatoes, water and spices. Simmer until potatoes are tender, about 15 minutes.
3. Purée in food processor, adding milk and half-and-half. Add salt and pepper to taste.
4. Pour back into soup pot and reheat gently.
5. Garnish with chopped parsley, if desired.

Makes 8 servings.

Each serving contains about: 270 calories, 6g protein, 35g carbohydrate, 4g fiber, 12g fat, 38mg cholesterol, 167mg sodium.

Sunshine Pudding

This light pudding resembles spoonbread, popular in southern states. The vegetables here add a splash of color and their own natural sweetness.

> 1 medium to large sweet potato, peeled, cooked and puréed to make
> ½ cup
> 2 medium carrots, scraped, cooked and puréed to make ½ cup
> 2 tablespoons brown sugar
> ½ cup bread crumbs
> 1¼ cups milk
> 1 large egg, well beaten

1. In a bowl combine potato, carrot, sugar and bread crumbs.
2. Whisk milk with egg and add to potato mixture.
3. Lightly coat a 1-quart baking dish with nonstick cooking spray, and pour in pudding mixture.
4. Bake at 350 degrees F for 1 hour.

Makes 4 servings.

Each serving contains about: 195 calories, 7g protein, 32g carbohydrate, 3g fiber, 5g fat, 64mg cholesterol, 165mg sodium.

Happy Yams

If you have a sweet tooth, candied yams on the Thanksgiving table are a must; this variation on the popular theme is a spirited one.

> 1 to 1½ lbs sweet potatoes ("yams")
> ¾ cup brown sugar
> ½ teaspoon salt
> ½ teaspoon grated orange peel
> 5 tablespoons butter or margarine
> ¼ to ⅓ cup light rum
> ½ cup chopped walnuts

1. Scrub sweet potatoes and boil until tender, but not soft. Cool slightly, peel, and slice about ½-inch thick.
2. Lightly coat a 10 x 7 x 2-inch baking dish with nonstick cooking spray.
3. Layer potatoes in dish alternately with sprinklings of brown sugar, salt, orange peel and butter.
4. Pour on rum and sprinkle with walnuts.
5. Bake at 350 degrees F for about 30 minutes, until hot and bubbly.

Makes 6 servings.

Each serving contains about: 352 calories, 3g protein, 47g carbohydrate, 3g fiber, 16g fat, 26mg cholesterol, 294mg sodium.

Sweet Potato-Apple Dessert

The fresh crops of sweet potatoes and the finest-flavored apples arrive in markets at about the same time in early fall. Here is a pretty dessert that combines them.

3 cups cooked sweet potatoes, peeled and cut in chunks
1 tablespoon brown sugar
1 tablespoon mild honey
3 tablespoons melted butter or margarine (divided)
2 large eggs, separated
3 red apples, peeled, cored and cut into 12 circular slices

1. In a food processor purée sweet potatoes, brown sugar, honey, 2 tablespoons of butter and egg yolks.
2. In a separate bowl whisk egg whites until stiff and peaks are formed. Fold into sweet-potato mixture.
3. Butter 6 custard cups, and place a slice of apple in the bottom of each cup. Divide mixture equally to fill cups, and place a slice of apple on top of mixture in each cup. Brush apple slices with remaining melted butter.
4. Place cups in a pan filled half-way up the sides with hot water.
5. Bake at 350 degrees F for 30 minutes.
6. Let cool 10 minutes, then run a knife around the sides of each cup. Invert on a plate and serve warm.

Makes 6 servings.

Each serving contains about: 210 calories, 3g protein, 33g carbohydrate, 3g fiber, 8g fat, 86mg cholesterol, 90mg sodium.

Holiday Pie

Company for the holidays! Be sure the desserts are special by including this one as a finale to the feasting.

    Pastry for a 9-inch pie shell (see recipe below)
    2 medium-size sweet potatoes
    2 large eggs
    ⅔ cup granulated sugar
    1 teaspoon *each* salt, ground cinnamon and vanilla extract
    ½ teaspoon ground cloves
    ¼ teaspoon *each* ground mace and ground ginger
    1 (5-oz) can evaporated milk, and sufficient fresh milk to make 1 cup
        total
    2 tablespoons brandy (or 1 teaspoon brandy extract)
    Whipped cream for topping (optional)

1. Make pastry.
2. Boil sweet potatoes until tender, remove skin. Should be about 1½ cups.
3. In food processor blend potatoes with eggs, sugar, and spices. Mix in milk and brandy. Pour into unbaked pastry shell.
4. Bake at 350 degrees F for 40 to 50 minutes, until toothpick inserted in center of pie comes out clean. Serve warm with whipped cream, if desired.

Pastry (single crust for one 9-inch pie)

    ½ cup (1 stick) margarine
    1 teaspoon granulated sugar
    ⅛ teaspoon salt
    1¼ cups unbleached all-purpose or pastry flour
    2 tablespoons ice water

Mix all ingredients. Chill in freezer for about ½ hour. Roll out and trim to fit 9-inch pie pan, giving edges a decorative finish with fingertips.

Makes one 9-inch pie, about 8 servings.

Each serving (without cream) contains about: 337 calories, 6g protein, 45g carbohydrate, 2g fiber, 15g fat, 60mg cholesterol, 499mg sodium.

T

Taro

(*Colocasio esculenta*)   See also Malanga.

Also known as: Eddo; Dasheen; Tannia.

History and lore: Beyond the highrises of Honolulu and the beaches of Waikiki, you still see Hawaiians in the quiet countryside tending their lush patches of taro plants. Taro-growing is an integral part of Hawaiian culture: When farmers instruct young people about the traditional way to cultivate taro, they also teach them elements of Hawaiian religion, myths and legends, and the remarkable knowledge the early Polynesians had about the wise use of their land.

Taro is probably native to southeast Asia, Malaysia and Indonesia, and has been spread by cultivation to Pacific islands, Japan, China and sixty other countries around the world. Plants taken to the West Indies by explorers in the 1500s were called dasheen, a name probably from French *de la Chine*, "from China."

Captain James Cook, who sampled taro throughout the Pacific, found it *"A very wholsome root."* When he arrived in Hawaii in 1778, the population (of around 300,000) depended on a diet of taro, sweet potato, fish and a few fruits.

Over 85 types of taro are grown in the Hawaiian Islands, but most of the crop is processed into poi (fermented or unfermented taro paste), and other products such as taro flour, bread, pastas, chips, pancake mix, baby food and *kulolo* (a popular Hawaiian confection).

Seasons when available: Year-round in Latin American or Oriental markets and some supermarkets.

What to look for when shopping: Buy firm, unblemished roots, avoiding any with cut skin or soft spots. Taro is brown, shaggy, barrel-shaped, circled with distinct rings; size is roughly like a turnip or rutabaga. Tiny rootlets usually twist from one end. Flesh may be white, cream or pale lilac in color, sometimes speckled with brown. The mild flavor is like a combination of potatoes and water chestnuts, or between artichoke hearts and chestnuts.

Nutritional highlights: High in potassium and fiber; low in sodium.

Amount for 4 servings: About 1 lb, one large root.

How to store: Taro will keep up to 2 weeks arranged in a single layer in a cool, dry place, but not the refrigerator. If you do refrigerate it, store only 3 or 4 days then use promptly.

Basic prep: *Never eat taro raw.* Before preparation, oil your hands or wear disposable gloves. All uncooked taro contains acrid calcium oxylate crystals severely irritating to the skin or mouth; the vegetable *must* be cooked to destroy these crystals. (Antidote, external: wash skin with a cold solution of water and salt; internal: sprinkle salt in the mouth and then spit out. Rinse with cold water. Repeat if necessary.)

Scrub root well. Slice off ends, pare deeply to remove all skin and discoloration; place at once in cold water.

To boil small taro, cover unpeeled roots with water and cook about 40 minutes or until soft. To bake them, place in a shallow pan of water, at 350 degrees F for 1½ hours.

Ways to serve: Taro can be baked, boiled, steamed or added to stir-fries. They take well to being deep-fried or pan-fried, made into lovely thin chips or strips. After being cooked, puréed taro makes ideal baby food and is good added to salads, fritters, biscuits, muffins and cakes.

Hilo Stew

Taro root substitutes for potato in this dish, and adds a distinctive sweetness. Seitan is a vegetable protein product made from wheat gluten, available in most health food or specialty markets. Mushroom bouillon is found in most supermarkets in the Jewish ethnic section.

1 large onion, diced
1 rib celery, chopped
1 garlic clove, minced
9 oz Seitan vegetable protein, cut into bite-size chunks
2 tablespoons butter or margarine
4 to 5 taro roots (about 1 cup) peeled and cut into chunks
4 oz fresh mushrooms
3 carrots, peeled and sliced
½ cup fresh peas
1 mushroom bouillon cube dissolved in 2 cups hot water
1 tablespoon tomato ketchup
1 teaspoon Worcestershire sauce

1. In a large stew pot, sauté onion, celery, garlic and Seitan chunks in butter, until onion is translucent.
2. Add taro and remaining vegetables.
3. Mix mushroom bouillon liquid with ketchup and Worcestershire sauce. Add to vegetables in stew pot.
4. Cover and simmer for about 1 hour, adding more water if necessary, as the taro absorbs the rich vegetable juices.
5. Ladle onto a bed of rice.

Makes 5 servings.

Each serving contains about: 151 calories, 10g protein, 18g carbohydrate, 4g fiber, 6g fat, 13mg cholesterol, 618mg sodium.

Taro Patties

These savory patties must be refrigerated before cooking, to hold their shape well. Serve them either as a side dish at dinner, or as a luncheon entrée with a crisp salad.

1½ lbs taro root, peeled
1 medium onion, diced
1 jalapeño chili pepper, seeded and minced
1 tablespoon cooking oil
¼ cup butter or margarine, melted
½ cup unbleached all-purpose flour
Oil for frying

1. Cover taro root with boiling water and cook 30 to 40 minutes, or until an inserted knife goes through and root is soft.
2. Sauté onion and jalapeño pepper in cooking oil until translucent, about 10 minutes.
3. Purée taro root in a food processor, and blend with onions, pepper and butter.
4. Form mixture into twelve 3-inch patties, ½ inch thick, and dust with flour.
5. Refrigerate at least 4 hours or overnight.
6. Fry patties in oil until golden brown on both sides.

Makes twelve 3-inch patties.

Each patty contains about: 177 calories, 2g protein, 20g carbohydrate, 2g fiber, 11g fat, 10mg cholesterol, 66mg sodium.

Maui Pancakes with Applesauce

Taro makes these pancakes special — just perfect for a leisurely Sunday brunch. Serve them hot, perhaps garnished with a dab of sour cream.

    2 fresh taro roots (about 2½ cups after grating)
    ½ small onion, finely minced
    1 large egg, well beaten
    ½ cup unbleached all-purpose flour
    ½ teaspoon seasoned salt
    Oil for frying (¼ to ½ cup)
    1½ cups applesauce
    Sour cream garnish (optional)

1. Use food processor to grate taro (should make about 2½ cups).
2. Boil in salted water for 5 minutes, and drain well.
3. In a medium bowl mix in onion, egg, flour and salt.
4. Heat oil. Drop spoonfuls of batter onto oiled pan and brown on both sides. Serve hot with applesauce.

Makes 4 servings.

Each serving (without sour cream) contains about: 312 calories, 5g protein, 41g carbohydrate, 4g fiber, 15g fat, 53mg cholesterol, 292mg sodium.

Turnip

(Brassica rapa)   See also its cousin, Rutabaga.

History and lore: The turnip probably originated in middle and eastern Asia, then spread by cultivation throughout temperate climates.

Fresh crops of young turnips are sweet, crisp and delicious, so it's a mistake to think this root is bitter and woody, perhaps because you have only eaten old oversized roots.

Contempt for the turnip as a lowly vegetable goes back centuries, maybe because it was so often a food for the poor. When proud Aryan tribes invaded the Indus Valley in the second millennium before Christ, their diet was beef, mutton, milk and curds; they prohibited their race from eating turnips, garlic, onions and beans because they considered them demeaning foods of the people they had conquered.

The Romans also may have thought them lowly, but they ate a lot of them; Pliny said turnips were the third most important crop north of the Po River, after wine and wheat; and from the ashes of Vesuvius archeologists have recovered a silver vase on which turnips are shown. Even in the Middle Ages, turnips were not always admired: before the tomato arrived in Europe, the turnip was the vegetable thrown at people as an insult, and English country lasses would present the root to a suitor when rejecting him.

In North America, Jacques Cartier planted turnip seeds in Canada in 1540, and as settlers moved west across the American continent, they took turnips with them all the way to the Northwest; they taught Indian women to bake or roast them whole as they had been doing with wild camas roots.

Seasons when available: Although sold all year in supermarkets, best time is between October and March. Best buys are early crops at farmers' markets in August.

What to look for when shopping: If green tops are still intact, their freshness is a good indication of the quality of the roots. Turnips should be firm, smooth and round. Look for *young* roots of small to medium size, about 2-inches diameter; very large turnips will probably be woody and bitter. Outer skin is white with purplish or greenish streaks. Raw turnips have a sweet peppery flavor; long cooking makes them taste strong.

Nutritional highlights: Low in calories, high in vitamin C and potassium. The turnip is one of the cruciferous vegetables believed to be a cancer preventive. Both roots and tops provide tasty nutrition.

Amount for 4 servings: 1 lb, about three medium. As well as bulk sales, turnips are often sold in 1 lb cello bags.

How to store: Cut off tops and refrigerate separately in plastic bag; use within 1 week. Store unwashed turnips in plastic bag; use within 10 days. Whole fully cooked turnips can be kept frozen in a plastic bag for about 8 months.

Basic prep: Cut off any tops but don't discard them; cook and serve those nutritious greens separately, as a source of calcium. The greens and their cooking liquid, "pot likker," is a favorite dish in Southern states said to cure hangovers. The tops are delicious sautéed with a little olive oil and garlic.

Scrub roots and pare thinly to reach the tender inner meat. Leave whole or cut into chunks. To boil, heat 1-inch water to boiling; add turnips. Cover and heat to boiling. Cook whole turnips 25 minutes, chunks 15 minutes, or until tender. Overcooking will make flavor and odor become undesirably stronger.

If you are sensitive to gas-forming foods, be cautious: eat small amounts of turnips at first to test how well you tolerate them, or use Beano or Be Sure products (directions on packages).

Ways to serve: Young turnips add a sweet-tasting crunch when diced raw in salads or cut into finger-shapes for appetizers. Turnips can be scalloped like potatoes; or glazed in hot melted butter, paprika and sugar; or mashed cooked turnips can be whisked with potatoes and apples (in any proportion) for the peasant-style dish, *Himmel und Erde.*

Smoky Turnip Soup

A warm and comforting soup for a chilly day, with the turnip flavor combining beautifully with brown rice, and accented by liquid smoke.

2 lbs small white turnips, peeled and quartered
1 medium onion, chopped
1 medium carrot, peeled and quartered
3 tablespoons butter or margarine
8 cups vegetable stock (see page 20), or vegetable bouillon (1 teaspoon
    or 1 cube for each cup water)
2 tablespoons fresh parsley, chopped
1 cup brown rice
2 tablespoons liquid-smoke seasoning
Salt and pepper to taste
½ cup freshly grated Parmesan cheese

1. Place turnips, onion and carrot in a large soup pot and sauté in butter.
2. Add stock and parsley, and simmer for about 15 minutes.
3. Add rice and liquid smoke, and cook another 20 minutes, or until
   turnips and rice are cooked and tender. Add salt and pepper.
4. Serve in soup bowls and sprinkle with Parmesan.

Makes 6 servings.

Each serving contains about: 300 calories, 9g protein, 44g carbohydrate,
5g fiber, 12g fat, 28mg cholesterol, 393mg sodium.

Turnip Puff Casserole

White turnips are available all year, so this lovely casserole can be made often, whatever the season.

    2 tablespoons butter or margarine
    ¼ cup minced onion
    2 tablespoons unbleached all-purpose flour
    3 cups mashed cooked turnips
    1 teaspoon salt
    2 teaspoons granulated sugar
    ⅛ teaspoon freshly ground black pepper
    2 large eggs, separated

1. Melt butter in a large pan, add onion and sauté until tender. Add flour and stir well to blend. Add turnips, salt, sugar, pepper and beaten egg yolks.
2. In a small bowl whisk egg whites until stiff, and fold into turnip mixture.
3. Pour into a buttered 2-quart casserole dish.
4. Bake at 350 degrees F for 40 minutes.

Makes 4 servings.

Each serving contains about: 135 calories, 5g protein, 12g carbohydrate, 3g fiber, 8g fat, 121mg cholesterol, 682mg sodium.

Turnip Custards

Savory root custards are easy to prepare and make lovely side dishes. Use roots other than turnips, if you like, such as small rutabagas, parsnips or baby carrots, depending on what is in season and the best quality.

1½ cups grated turnips
3 cups milk, scalded
3 large eggs, well beaten
½ teaspoon freshly ground black pepper
⅛ teaspoon freshly ground nutmeg
2 tablespoons grated onion
2 tablespoons chopped green bell pepper
1 tablespoon finely chopped fresh parsley
4 tablespoons butter or margarine, melted

1. In a large bowl, stir turnips and milk into the eggs; add pepper and nutmeg. Beat until foamy.
2. Add onion, bell pepper, parsley and melted butter. Mix till well blended, and pour into 6 buttered custard cups.
3. Place cups in a 13 x 9 x 2-inch pan. Pour hot water in pan to within ½ inch of the top of the cups.
4. Bake at 350 degrees F for 40 to 45 minutes, or until a knife inserted in centers comes out clean.

Makes 6 servings.

Each serving contains about: 191 calories, 8g protein, 9g carbohydrate, 1g fiber, 14g fat, 143mg cholesterol, 191mg sodium.

Mint-Glazed Turnips

While on a cruise, Sandra was introduced to the intriguing sharp-sweet flavors of a delectable turnip dish. The chef generously sent the recipe, which is beautifully simple.

 2 lbs turnips, peeled and quartered
 ½ cup white vinegar
 4 tablespoons powdered sugar
 ¼ cup finely chopped fresh mint leaves

1. Cook turnips in boiling water, about 20 minutes until tender. Drain.
2. In a separate pan, heat vinegar and sugar, and stir till blended. Put chopped mint in a bowl and pour vinegar-sugar mixture over the mint. Let stand about 1 hour.
3. Put turnips in a shallow pan and add mint mixture.
4. Bake at 350 degrees F for about 15 minutes, or until well glazed.

Makes 4 servings.

Each serving contains about: 91 calories, 2g protein, 22g carbohydrate, 4g fiber, 1g fat, 0mg cholesterol, 154mg sodium.

Turnip Nests with Glazed Pearl Onions

A flavorful combination: the onions give a sweetness to the peppery vegetable. Mock-chicken granules are sold in health-food stores; dissolve 1 teaspoon granules in 1 cup water.

> 4 medium size turnips, peeled
> 3 tablespoons butter or margarine
> 1 cup mock-chicken broth
> 2 tablespoons granulated sugar
> ½ lb pearl onions, peeled
> ⅓ cup chopped fresh chives for garnish

1. Cut bottoms off turnips so they sit level on a plate. Carefully scoop center from each turnip (saving pulp for another use — perhaps a salad topping).
2. Melt butter and add turnips, browning on all sides. Add mock-chicken broth and simmer for about 10 minutes, till turnips are tender. Remove turnips and save broth.
3. In a saucepan, dissolve sugar in ¼ cup reserved broth. Just before sugar colors and caramelizes, add onions and more broth if necessary. Cook for about 2 more minutes.
4. Fill turnips with onions and sprinkle with chives. Serve hot.

Makes 4 servings.

Each serving contains about: 157 calories, 2g protein, 19g carbohydrate, 3g fiber, 9g fat, 23mg cholesterol, 446mg sodium.

Water chestnut

(Eleocharis dulcis)

Also known as: Chinese water chestnut.

History and lore: Where would we be without water chestnuts in chop suey, rumaki or spinach salad? Yet Americans usually only consider the bland ones in cans that are more readily-available. Oriental groceries sell fresh water chestnuts, and their flavor is unbelievable. Once tried, you won't settle again for canned.

Water chestnuts grow in mud along the edges of ponds, lakes and marshes; although they look like chestnuts they are really corms, planted like flower bulbs. As you'd expect, they are widely grown in China and southeast Asia, and have been since prehistory. At "Spirit Cave" in Thailand, archeologists have found remains of their cultivation dating back to 9750 B.C.

Although most supplies of fresh water chestnuts are at present imported from China and Taiwan, small experimental farms in California and southern states in America are increasing their crops.

Seasons when available: Year-round.

What to look for when shopping: Like muddy chestnuts, about 1!/2 inches diameter, the tulip-like bulbs have thin dark-brown skins with frayed leaf scales. Corms should be rock-hard; avoid any with shrivelled or soft decayed spots. After peeling, the flesh is white. Raw fresh water chestnuts are crisp with a sweet flavor somewhere between jicama, coconut and a tart apple. When cooked, the smell and flavor is like nutty sweet corn.

Some markets sell ready-peeled water chestnuts in shallow tanks of water in the produce section.

Large supermarkets sell canned water chestnuts, available all year in the Oriental section.

Nutritional highlights: Low in calories and sodium; high in potassium; some B vitamins.

Amount for 4 servings: ½ lb bulbs (peeling results in much wastage).

How to store: Wrap unwashed chestnuts in a paper sack and store in coldest part of refrigerator. Don't remove any mud as it prevents drying out. Or place unwashed bulbs in a jar of water and refrigerate; they lose some flavor but will stay crisp and fresh. Use within 2 weeks.

Freeze unwashed, unpeeled water chestnuts in a plastic bag.

Basic prep: Scrub well to remove any mud. Peel them, discard any brown spots, and place bulbs in a small bowl of water with a few drops of lemon juice, to keep flesh white. Cut water chestnuts into halves, quarters, coin slices, dice or julienne strips.

Brief cooking will enhance flavor of whole bulbs: about 10 minutes in fresh boiling water.

Ways to serve: Use raw to add a delicious crunch to crisp green salad, spinach salad, watercress salad, fruit salad, relish trays or salsas. Add small dice to stir-fries, chop suey, soups, casseroles and side dishes of rice or pastas. Or simply serve them as a hot vegetable, with a little melted butter, salt and pepper.

Hot and Sour Soup

This Szechwan-style soup is a delicious start to any Chinese meal. White pepper makes it hot, vinegar makes it sour, and dried black mushrooms give an authentic flavor. The latter are sold in Oriental groceries and most large super-markets; if unavailable in your area, substitute an 8-oz can of regular mush-rooms.

4 to 6 dried black mushrooms, or 1 (8-oz) can mushrooms
4 cups vegetable stock (see page 20), or vegetable bouillon (1 teaspoon or 1 cube for each cup water)
1 tablespoon Sherry
½ cup sliced fresh water chestnuts
4 oz firm tofu, diced
2 tablespoons white vinegar
1½ teaspoons soy sauce
½ teaspoon white pepper
2 tablespoons cornstarch
¼ cup cold water
1 large egg
1 scallion, minced
½ teaspoon sesame oil

1. Soak dried mushrooms in enough liquid to cover; save liquid and add to stock. Ignore this step if using canned mushrooms.
2. Place stock in a 2-quart saucepan and add slivered mushrooms, Sherry and water chestnuts. Bring to a boil, and simmer for 10 minutes.
3. Add tofu, vinegar, soy sauce and pepper.
4. Blend cornstarch and water, and add to soup. Cook and stir until slightly thickened.
5. Beat egg lightly, and slowly pour it into soup. Heat for 1 minute.
6. Sprinkle with scallion and sesame oil.

Makes 6 servings.

Each serving contains about: 87 calories, 4g protein, 11g carbohydrate, 1g fiber, 4g fat, 38mg cholesterol, 296mg sodium.

Thai Noodle Salad

This cool refreshing main-dish salad has a blend of textures and flavors from southeast Asia. Be sure to top with chopped roasted peanuts for an authentic touch. The Oriental-style noodles can be found in Asian markets and some supermarkets.

> 1 (16-oz) package Tomoshiraga Somen (Japanese alimentary paste)
> Dressing (see recipe below)
> 8 oz fresh peeled water chestnuts, or 1 (8-oz) can sliced water chestnuts, drained
> 1 cup carrots, peeled and cut into julienne strips
> 1 cup red or yellow bell peppers, cubed
> 1 cup snow peas, cut in half
> ½ cup chopped scallions (bite-size diagonal pieces)
> Salad greens
> ¾ cup chopped roasted peanuts

1. Cook noodles according to directions on package. Drain and cool completely.
2. Mix dressing in a small bowl.
3. In a separate bowl, combine remaining ingredients except salad greens and peanuts.
4. Arrange salad greens on 6 plates.
5. Toss noodles, vegetables and dressing together, and spoon onto salad greens. Top with roasted peanuts and serve cold.

Dressing (makes about 1½ cups)

> 1½ tablespoons fresh basil
> 1 tablespoon fresh mint leaves, crushed
> 1 cup coconut milk
> 1 tablespoon sesame or peanut oil
> 1 tablespoon grated fresh ginger root
> 2 garlic cloves, minced
> 2 tablespoons fresh lemon juice

Combine all ingredients in a small bowl and set aside to chill.

Makes 6 servings.

Each serving contains about: 399 calories, 11g protein, 44g carbohydrate, 6g fiber, 22g fat, 0mg cholesterol, 25mg sodium.

Shanghai Salad

This unusual salad, crisp and colorful, makes a perfect luncheon on a hot day. Make the light dressing the day before, if possible, so flavors have time to blend thoroughly. Increase the curry powder if you like more spiciness.

Dressing (see recipe below)
½ cup fresh water chestnuts, sliced
2 cups fresh bean sprouts, washed and drained
½ cup green seedless grapes, halved if large
⅓ cup finely diced red bell pepper
1 large nectarine, seeded and cut small

1. Mix dressing and set aside to chill.
2. Combine salad ingredients in a medium bowl.
3. Pour dressing over salad. Toss and serve.

Dressing (makes about ⅔ cup)

½ cup plain yogurt
1½ teaspoons curry powder
1 teaspoon soy sauce
½ teaspoon granulated sugar
1 teaspoon garlic powder

Mix yogurt, curry, soy sauce, sugar and garlic powder in a small bowl, and chill thoroughly.

Makes 4 servings.

Each serving contains about: 91 calories, 4g protein, 18g carbohydrate, 3g fiber, 1g fat, 2mg cholesterol, 112mg sodium.

Roots Calendar

	JAN	FEB	MAR	APR	MAY	JUN	JUL	AUG	SEP	OCT	NOV	DEC
Arrowroot	X	X	X	X	X	X	X	X	X	X	X	X
Beet	X	X	X	X	X	●	●	X	X	X	X	X
Boniato	X	X	X	X	X	X	X	X	X	X	X	X
Carrot	X	X	X	X	X	X	X	X	X	X	X	X
Cassava (Yuca)	X	X	X	X	X	X	X	X	X	X	X	X
Celeriac (Celery root)	X	X	X	X	X			X	X	●	●	X
Daikon (Lo bok)	X	X	X	X	X	X	X	X	X	X	X	X
Fennel (Anise)	X	X	X							X	X	X
Garlic	X	X	X	X	X	X	X	X	X	X	X	X
Ginger	X	X	X	X	X	X	X	X	X	X	X	X
Gobo root (Burdock)	X	X	X	X	X	X	X	X	X	X	X	X
Horseradish	●	●	●	X	X	X	X	X	X	X	●	●
Jerusalem artichoke	X	X	X	X						X	X	X
Jicama	X	X	X	X	X	X	X	X	X	X	X	X
Kohlrabi	X	X	X	X	●	●	X	X	X	X	X	X
Leek	●	●	●	●	●	●	X	X	X	X	●	●
Lotus root, fresh	X	X								X	X	X
Malanga	X	X	X	X	X	X	X	X	X	X	X	X
Onion	X	X	X	X	X	X	X	X	X	X	X	X
Parsley root	●	X	X	X				X	X	X	X	X
Parsnip	●	●	X	X	X	X	X	X	X	X	X	●
Potato	X	X	X	X	X	X	X	X	X	X	X	X
Radish	X	X	X	X	X	X	X	X	X	X	X	X
Rutabaga	X	X								X	X	X
Salsify (Oyster plant)	X	X	X	X						X	X	X
Scallion (Green onion)	X	X	X	X	X	X	X	X	X	X	X	X
Shallot	X	X	X	X	X	X	X	X	X	X	X	X
Sweet potato (Yam)	●	X	X	X	X	X	X	X	X	●	●	●
Taro	X	X	X	X	X	X	X	X	X	X	X	X
Turnip	●	●	●	X	X	X	X	X	X	●	●	●
Water chestnut	X	X	X	X	X	X	X	X	X	X	X	X

X = AVAILABLE   ● = PEAK SEASON

Appendix 2
Major Nutrients in Roots

	Serving size	Weight g	Calories	Protein g	Carb g
Arrowroot, powdered	1 oz	28	103	0.1	25
Beet, diced, cooked	½ cup	85	26	0.9	6
Boniato, raw	½ cup	N/A	90	1.0	20
Carrot, raw, grated	½ cup	55	24	0.6	6
Cassava, fresh	½ cup	78	94	2.4	21
Celeriac, cooked	½ cup	75	19	0.7	4
Daikon, raw	½ cup	44	8	0.3	2
Fennel, raw, chopped	¾ cup	100	15	1.1	3
Garlic clove, fresh	1 clove	3	5	0.2	1
Ginger, raw, sliced	5 slices	11	8	0.2	2
Gobo root, raw	½ cup	59	42	0.9	10
Horseradish, raw, grated	1 tblsp	15	13	0.5	3
Jerusalem artichoke, raw	½ cup	75	57	1.5	13
Jicama, raw	½ cup	60	24	0.8	5
Kohlrabi, raw, sliced	½ cup	70	19	1.2	4
Leek, raw, chopped	½ cup	52	32	0.8	7
Lotus root, raw, sliced	5 slices	40	23	1.0	7
Malanga, raw	½ cup	75	137	2.2	32
Onion, raw, chopped	½ cup	80	30	0.9	7
Parsley root, raw, chopped	¾ cup	100	37	2.9	5
Parsnip, raw, sliced	½ cup	66	50	0.8	12
Potato, peeled, boiled	1 each	135	116	2.3	27
Radish, raw	5 each	22	4	0.1	1
Rutabaga, raw, cubed	½ cup	70	25	0.8	6
Salsify, boiled	½ cup	67	46	1.8	10
Scallion, raw, chopped	½ cup	50	16	0.9	4
Shallot, raw, chopped	½ cup	80	58	2.0	13
Sweet potato, peeled, boiled	1 each	151	158	2.5	37
Taro, cooked, sliced	½ cup	66	93	0.3	23
Turnip, raw, cubed	½ cup	65	18	0.6	4
Water chestnut, fresh, raw	½ cup	62	66	0.9	15

Fiber g	Calcium mg	Iron mg	Sodium mg	Potassium mg	
0.1	2	0.56	5	2	Arrowroot
1.7	9	0.53	42	265	Beet
1.0	N/A	N/A	7	612	Boniato
1.8	15	0.28	19	177	Carrot
3.7	71	2.81	6	596	Cassava
3.7	19	0.32	46	130	Celeriac
1.0	12	0.18	9	100	Daikon
1.0	44	0.80	90	330	Fennel
0.1	5	0.05	1	12	Garlic
0.1	2	0.05	1	46	Ginger
1.1	24	0.47	3	181	Gobo root
0.3	21	0.21	1	85	Horseradish
1.0	10	2.55	3	321	Jerusalem art.
0.5	9	0.36	3	105	Jicama
1.0	17	0.28	14	245	Kohlrabi
1.2	31	1.09	10	93	Leek
0.3	18	0.47	16	225	Lotus root
2.0	16	0.90	N/A	N/A	Malanga
1.3	16	0.18	2	125	Onion
4.0	1	0.85	12	399	Parsley root
3.0	24	0.39	7	249	Parsnip
2.0	11	0.42	7	442	Potato
0.5	5	0.06	5	52	Radish
1.0	33	0.36	14	235	Rutabaga
1.5	32	0.37	11	191	Salsify
1.2	36	0.74	8	138	Scallion
0.6	30	0.96	10	267	Shallot
4.5	32	0.85	20	277	Sweet potato
2.5	12	0.47	10	319	Taro
1.2	19	0.19	44	124	Turnip
1.9	7	0.04	9	362	Water chestnut

NOTES: 1. Roots are essentially fat free, containing trace amounts (less than 0.5g/100g).
2. Vitamin A is an important nutrient in carrots and sweet potatoes.

Selected References

Allen, Betty. *Legends of Old Hawaii*. Honolulu, Hawaii: Tongg Publishing Company, Ltd., 1944 (1957 edition).

Francatelli, Charles Elmé. *A Plain Cookery Book for the Working Classes*. London, England: Routledge, Warne and Routledge, 1852.

Gray, William R. *Voyages to Paradise: Exploring in the Wake of Captain Cook*. Washington, D.C.: National Geographic Society, 1981.

Masefield G.B. et al. *The Oxford Book of Food Plants*. London, England: Oxford University Press, 1969.

McGee, Harold. *On Food and Cooking*. New York, New York: Charles Scribner's Sons, 1984.

Pukui, Mary Kawena. *Pikoi and other Legends of the Island of Hawaii*. Honolulu, Hawaii: Kamehameha Schools Press, 1949.

Root, Waverley. *Food*. New York, New York: Simon & Schuster, 1980.

Schneider, Elizabeth. *Uncommon Fruits and Vegetables*. New York, New York: Harper & Row, Publishers, 1986.

Tannahill, Reay. *Food in History*. New York, New York: Stein and Day Publishers, 1973.

Weiner, Michael A. *Earth Medicine—Earth Foods*. New York, New York: Macmillan Publishing Co. Inc., 1972.

Index of Recipes

❀ Vegan

Appetizers, Snacks and Nibbles

Soups, Broths and Stock

Salads

Cakes

Blush Cake, 35
❋ Chocolate Carrot Cake, 45
Ginger Pound Cake with Apricot-Orange Sauce, 79

Breads, Cookies and Crackers

Arrowroot Lemon Cookies, 25
Banana Arrowroot Muffins, 28
Beet Date Bread, 34
Jill's Skinny Scallion Crackers, 167
Onion Biscuits, 123
Shallot-Butter Garlic Bread, 172

Pickles and Relishes

❋ Pickled Daikon, 61
❋ Rosy Relish, 88
❋ Spicy Radish Relish, 151

Sauces and Salsas

Apricot-Orange Sauce, 79
Horseradish Sauce #1 (with scallions), 86
Horseradish Sauce #2 (with egg yolks), 86
Horseradish Sauce #3 (cream style), 87
❋ Jicama Salsa, 96
Onion-Mushroom Sauce, 141
Potato Garlic Sauce, 146

Index